Going from We to Me

Going from We to Me:

A Financial Guide to Divorce

By Adrienne Rothstein Grace,
CFP®, CDFA™
Certified Divorce Financial Analyst

Going from 'We to Me': A Financial Guide to Divorce
Copyright © 2019 Adrienne Rothstein Grace, Certified Divorce Financial Analyst™, Certified Financial Planner®

BMD Publishing
All Rights Reserved
1st Edition 2016
ISBN # 978-1534698437

BMDPublishing@MarketDominationLLC.com
MarketDominationLLC.com

BMD Publishing CEO: Seth Greene
Editorial Management: Bruce Corris
Technical Editor & Layout: Kristin Watt

While great care was taken to prepare this book, it is not a substitute for legal, financial, medical or other professional advice based on your specific circumstances. Consult with an experienced Family Law Attorney, Mediator, Accountant, Certified Financial Planner® (CFP®), and Certified Divorce Financial Analyst™ (CDFA™) about your specific case. While the author of this book is a Certified Financial Planner® and a Certified Divorce Financial Analyst™, in this book she is not dispensing financial advice based on your own situation, or legal advice either directly or indirectly. The intent of this book is to help you move through your divorce and avoid becoming a financial victim of your decisions and those of your spouse. Under no circumstances will Adrienne Rothstein Grace or any of her representatives be liable for any special or consequential damages that result from the use of, or the inability to use, the information or strategies communicated through these materials, or any services provided prior to or following the receipt of these materials, even if advised of the possibility of such damages. You alone are responsible and accountable for your decisions, actions and results in life. By your use of these materials, you agree not to attempt to hold Adrienne Rothstein Grace liable for any such decisions, actions, or results, at any time, under any circumstances.

Printed in the United States of America

ACKNOWLEDGMENTS

To my clients, who provide the inspiration and the models for this book.

To Seth Greene, of www.MarketDominationLLC.com, who planted the idea that I could write a book, and helped bring it to reality.

With gratitude to my best friend, lover, reader and fact-checker whose patience while this book was being created helped make it possible. Thank you for being living proof that there is life and love after divorce

INTRODUCTION

Going from We to Me: A Financial Guide to Divorce ©

Marriage is about love; divorce is about money

Divorce.

It's one of the most difficult things anyone can go through.

It's a time of great pain...and great uncertainty.

Your life won't be the same.

I believe everyone should live a secure, confident and empowered financial life.

My clients are smart, strong capable people, who find themselves suddenly single. "Going from We to Me", they share the same concerns:

Will I Be Okay?

Can I be secure financially, for myself and my children?

My focus is helping you to move forward in the best way possible, to financial security and confidence, for now and for the future.

I understand the emotional roller coaster, the fear and uncertainty of this time. I know what a long road it can be- and that there can be a fulfilling new life at the other end. I have taken this journey myself. Now I help others to find their way.

I have helped hundreds of women have a more secure financial life.

You can have one, too.

This book is meant to be a practical guide, with steps you can take now to prepare for your divorce, get through it in the most positive and informed way possible, and achieve a reasonable and fair settlement that you can live with, both now and in the future.

Divorces are often about the past, filled with fear, anger and guilt. *Who did or failed to do what to whom? Who made the most or the least money? Who spent it, how and on what?* Promises are unfulfilled, expectations remain unmet, plans you may have taken for granted for the rest of your life are not going to happen. Distress, betrayal, shock, loss, anger, grief- all are normal and natural feelings at this time. Your daily life and routines change. This all shocks your world, and upsets your reasoning. The emotional impact of this situation often makes for really bad decision making.

Money issues are at the top of many couples' problem list. A study titled *Examining the Relationship between Financial Issues and Divorce* (1) examined what couples argue about -

and found that for men, arguments about money were the primary predictor of divorce. For women, it was arguments about both money and sex. Is this true for you?

Now, perhaps more than at any other time in your life, you need to think clearly about money and your financial future. Decisions you make now will affect the quality of your lifestyle and that of your children. Research consistently estimates that income in a divorcing household drops by as much as 30% on average. More than half of custodial parents don't receive payment of child support, in full or on time, as promised. This impact can last a lifetime.

Divorce also hurts the wealthy. Complex and hard to value assets, like closely-held businesses, commercial properties, professional practices, etc. make it very challenging for the non-financial spouse to get fair value in a settlement.

A word about guilt:

In the ending of any marriage, there is enough fault and blame to go around. If you were the one who had an affair, or did something else to damage the relationship, your first instinct is often to give up your financial interest in the settlement. Please don't. Your divorce settlement is not the best way to expiate the 'sins' committed during your relationship. Don't let your emotions get in the way of securing a financial future for you and your children. If you feel you were the injured party, keep in mind that a divorce is not an effective way to exact retribution either. Therapy can help you deal with these issues. Secure your finances, and then deal with the rest.

This book will help you focus on the future, and will help you answer this critical question: *"How can I be sure I will be financially secure after my divorce?"*

I strongly recommend, and therefore will assume in this book, that you have retained - or plan to retain - the services of an attorney to help you through this process. Whether you plan to Mediate, Collaborate or Litigate, a family law attorney's assistance is invaluable to help ensure that you are fully informed and your rights are fully protected. Your divorce settlement will shape your financial future. Consult an expert. The attorney who helped you to purchase your last home may not have the specialized skills to take you through this complex and critical journey. Divorce is expensive- consider the cost as an investment in your future. Choose your team wisely. This is not the time to automatically go to the lowest cost provider.

Domestic violence:

First of all- it's not your fault.

One in four relationships carries some form of abuse. Domestic abuse recognizes no economic or educational boundaries. Abuse- physical, emotional, mental, or financial- can be found in homes large and small, regardless of wealth, education, neighborhood, or ethnicity. Abuse victims are everywhere. It takes strength and courage to stand up for yourself and your children and say, "No more." If you are in this situation, please put this book down and pick up the phone. Contact your local domestic violence shelter, or call the National Domestic Violence Hotline at 1-800-799-SAFE (7233) for immediate help in your area. Help is available in English, Spanish, and 170 other languages through interpreters.

Then come back and learn more about how to avoid becoming a financial victim of your divorce. To help guide you through all the information here, we've noted 'What you will learn in this chapter' at the beginning of each one.

An Attorney can help you understand your rights under the law, and ensure that your interests are protected. A Mediator can help you and your spouse craft a divorce agreement to meet the needs of your family, out of court. A Marriage and Family Therapist can help you understand your emotions, help your children cope with these changes, and help everyone move on to the next phase of life. A Certified Divorce Financial Analyst™ can best help you evaluate and plan for the short and long-term financial consequences of your separation and divorce. Other specialists, depending upon your specific situation, may also be needed to help you get a fair and reasonable settlement that you and your family can live with. These people form your divorce team. *You don't have to do this alone.*

Note: he/she, his/her are used interchangeably in this book. When the text refers to husband, it could apply equally well to wife, and vice versa. These rules apply to same-gender couples as well.

(1)   *Family Relations Journal* (v. 61, No. 4, Oct. 2012), looked at data for 4,574 couples as part of the U.S. based "National Survey of Families and Households"

TABLE OF CONTENTS

ACKNOWLEDGMENTS v

INTRODUCTION vii

CHAPTER 1: What is Divorce? 1

CHAPTER 2: Being Prepared 7

CHAPTER 3: Choosing the Right Divorce Process 27

CHAPTER 4: How Much Will I Need? 47

CHAPTER 5: Can I Keep the House? 63

CHAPTER 6: Is 50/50 Fair? Or Which Half You Get Makes All the Difference 89

CHAPTER 7: Can I Keep My Pension? 111

CHAPTER 8: Alimony 125

CHAPTER 9: Child Support...143

CHAPTER 10: Insurance: Guaranteeing Child Support and Alimony 153

CHAPTER 11: Debt..167

CHAPTER 12: Is Your Spouse Hiding Assets? 181

CHAPTER 13: Building A Divorce Team 197

CHAPTER 14: How Much Will it Cost? 213

CLOSING THOUGHTS 223

APPENDIX: DOCUMENT CHECKLIST 227

CHAPTER 1

WHAT IS DIVORCE?

What you will learn:

The background of divorce;
The difference between divorce and legal separation;
The impact of different state laws.

Rosanna sighed deeply. She was exhausted after spending yet another night worrying about the future. Her marriage was long over, but how would she be able to get by without her husband? How would she pay the bills, put food on the table? He had always brought home a paycheck, while she stayed home and raised their children. "What shall I do?" she thought for the thousandth time.

First of all, take a deep breath. I understand that this may not be where you thought your life and your marriage would go. You built your life as a loving partnership, but it hasn't worked out. The reasons why are not the focus of this book- helping you to move forward in the best way possible is what we want to achieve.

As you start down this road, it's good to know exactly what we are talking about. Dissolving your marriage can involve several steps: living separately, a legal separation, annulment, and a legal divorce. Each choice may meet the needs of some couples, at some time. Feel free to discuss each one with your team of advisors. In this book, we'll deal primarily with the financial issues of a legal separation and a legal divorce.

If you are clear that you don't want to continue living with your spouse, but you are not certain that you want a divorce, then a legal separation may be the answer for now. You will have to negotiate child custody, support and a parenting plan, allmony and the division of property, just like in a divorce. There are several fine points of difference, but we can say that the key difference between legal separation and divorce is although you live your lives separately, you are still legally married. You are free to do many things on your own, but you may not remarry until you are legally divorced. If you later decide to go forward with a divorce, you will have to go through a legal process to officially terminate the marriage.

Why would you choose legal separation vs divorce? Here are a few common reasons:

1. You and/or your spouse are opposed to divorce for religious or moral reasons.
2. You or your spouse will remain eligible for the other's health insurance coverage only while married. Please check the policy carefully. Some insurance carriers will specifically exclude legally separated spouses from coverage. (See Chapter 10, Insurance for more information).
3. You have not yet met your state's residency requirements to be eligible for divorce where you live, but want a legal

separation agreement to protect your rights until you can file.
4. There are tax benefits for filing income tax as married.
5. Negotiating a separation agreement may be less stressful than negotiating a divorce.

You may consider an informal trial separation but if you plan to live apart for any substantial period of time, a formal, written separation agreement can protect you.

How will joint bills be paid? Who will be responsible for maintaining the house? Did you know that, even though you may be living apart, you can still be liable for your spouse's debts or legal issues?

Communication between the two of you may deteriorate during a long separation. Income could change, assets bought or sold, or funds mismanaged without your knowledge. A written legal separation agreement, stating each spouse's rights and responsibilities, division of property and support, can protect your interests and those of your children.

There are many legal and financial ramifications of legal separation. Be sure to consult a family law attorney for clarification of the legal matters, and a CDFA™ and/or a CPA for the financial issues.

Divorce is a legal action that ends a marriage before the death of either spouse and dissolves the bonds of matrimony between a husband and wife. A divorce decree establishes the new relationship between the former spouses, details their duties and obligations relating to property they own (division of property), support responsibilities to each other (alimony/maintenance), and provisions for any children (child custody and support).

How you arrive at these crucial agreements can shape your future and that of your children. Helping you avoid becoming a financial victim of this process is the goal of this book.

In early civilizations, marrying and ending a marriage were considered private matters, to be handled within families and communities.

Now, divorce laws vary considerably around the world, but most require the sanction of a court or other authority in a legal process. Divorce is recognized just about everywhere, with the exception of the Philippines and the Vatican City State.

In the United States, the laws of the state where you live govern your divorce. So they may be different where you live now, from where you were married. The only way you can get a divorce is through the state, so under the due process clause of the Fourteenth Amendment to the U.S. Constitution, a state must make divorce available to everyone, and must acknowledge a divorce granted in another state. This is a particularly important issue for military divorces, and for same gender couples. This means that divorce law consists of 51 different sets of conditions—one for each state and one for the District of Columbia. To meet residency requirements, you must live in the state where you are filing for a specified period of time. For example, you must live in Nevada for six weeks, in Arizona for 90 days, and in New Jersey for one year, to be able to file for divorce there.

If someone who wants a divorce can't afford the court expenses, filing fees, and other costs, they may file free of charge. Most states offer Mediation as an alternative to court appearance. The Collaborative process is available as well. We will discuss these alternatives in detail in Chapter 3.

All states now recognize no-fault divorce, since New York did so in 2010. Alaska, California and Nevada had begun this procedure as early as the 1960's. Before no-fault, you had to prove 'grounds' for the divorce. Cruelty, abandonment, adultery, nonsupport, alcoholism, drug addiction, insanity, criminal conviction, and voluntary separation were all traditional grounds for divorce. In 1933, New Mexico was the first state to also recognize 'incompatibility' as grounds. No-fault allows a couple to divorce without having to prove that your spouse did something wrong. Practically speaking, you can unilaterally decide that your marriage has irretrievably broken down, ('irreconcilable differences') and file for divorce. It still takes two to marry; <u>it takes only one to divorce</u>. The other spouse does not need to consent or agree - which introduces many pros and cons.

On the 'pro' side, couples do not need to remain locked in an abusive or unfulfilling relationship. Divorces can take place with less conflict than when 'fault' had to be proven. Divorce settlements can be based more on need, ability to pay, and contribution to the family finances, than on fault or wrongdoing.

On the 'con' side, no-fault removes control over saving the marriage. In a unilateral filing, one spouse files, and the other spouse cannot defend the marriage.

Indeed, 'marital misconduct' may not impact the judgment and division of property, depending on where you live. If your spouse was unfaithful and you were not, you will not automatically get a larger settlement. Most courts ignore 'bad behavior' (marital fault in legal terms) in granting settlement awards and instead use formulas as a basis for calculating child support and maintenance.

Historically, when a divorce was granted, the resolution was simple: The wife was awarded custody of the children, if any, and the husband was required to continue providing support for his ex-wife and children. Gender equality, the changing nature of the family, and the growing role of women in the workforce now impact these decisions. Depending on their circumstances, joint custody, or even sole custody of children can be granted to the father, and some women must pay alimony to their ex-husbands. The best way to deal with these situations is simple. Simple, but not easy: Be prepared.

CHAPTER 2

BEING PREPARED

What you will learn:

Practical tips to protect yourself and your children before filing or during the divorce process.

There's a lot of information here, much of which may pertain to your particular situation.
You may want to take notes on action items you can do now.

Ok, she thought. I have to do this. Living in limbo like this is not good for me, and it's not good for the children. What do I do next? How do I prepare so I'll be ready to move on? What can I do to protect myself and the kids, before I have to tell him that it's over? I'm really scared! I trusted him to take care of us, but now 'We' is just 'Me'- and I don't know where to start!

Whether you were a Scout or not, their motto still stands: "Be Prepared". When divorce is ahead, there are many things to do to get properly informed about your financial position. Especially if you were not the 'financial' spouse, the one who managed the household accounts and investments, you need to know as much about your finances as possible. Now the focus shifts from 'We' to 'Me'. This will be true for each of you. Keep that in mind in your discussions with your soon-to-be ex.

You don't have to do this alone. Your team can be made up of your attorney, mediator, therapist or counselor, and divorce financial analyst. Be sure to inform your advisor(s) of any written Pre-Marital Agreement (pre-nup). We'll talk more about choosing your attorney and/or mediator later.

Now is when having a Certified Divorce Financial Analyst™ (CDFA™) can be the most helpful. Your 'regular' financial advisor may not have the specialized knowledge and experience to help you through this troubled time. If he worked for you and your spouse together, a conflict of interest may be present as well. A CDFA™ can help you put together your financial and budget profile before you see your attorney, and likely save thousands of dollars in legal fees. A CDFA™ is specially equipped to help you craft creative solutions, and to project future values so that you can answer the question, '*Will I be OK?*' for now, and for later, too.

Here are some practical tips to help get you through.

Let's take care of you, first.

1. Establish Ways to Communicate Privately

You may want to keep your communication private, especially if you are preparing *before* having the 'big conversation' with your spouse. Set up a new postal mailing address for your private correspondence and bank statements. Rent a post office box if you can, or engage a trusted friend or family member to receive your mail.

Set up a new email account, using terms that are not familiar or immediately recognizable. If your current account is Liza57@aol.com, do NOT use Liza57@gmail.com! Avoid passwords you have used before and may have shared with your partner. Choose entirely new names and new passwords and follow the guidelines for more secure choices: capitalized and lower case letters, numbers that are not your birthdate and address, and when permitted, symbols. Don't write them down and leave them where they might be easily found. Have some fun with your new account name. For example, try something positive, like: 4Good*Days; NewChoices!4me; *MyNewLife1$; Fit&Fabulous45. Do the same with your passwords. Avoid children's birthdates, house numbers, social security numbers, or previously used passwords. Experts suggest that you use numbers to spell out a phrase: m3fr$T4Onc3. (Did you figure it out? "Me first for once").

The Decision:

Alice had finally decided that it was time for a divorce from Rob. Things had been so bad for so long. There was so much drama at home that it was hard to get through the evening, let alone the night. 'I'm so glad I have a job', she thought. Work is the one place where I don't have to think about the mess that my personal life has become.

If you're concerned about the privacy of your home computer, or if you don't have one, keep in mind that free use of computers is available at most public libraries. Try to avoid using your work computer for communication with your team, and your soon-to-be-ex, as email messages at work can legally be monitored by your supervisors. If you are working, do the best job you can. Your own income will continue to be important as you move forward with your divorce.

Put a password on your phone so your call history and text messages can't be accessed without it. As above, don't use your birthday, kids' birthdays or address as your password. Choose something positive and new. Then you can store your list of new accounts and passwords in your phone. If you are concerned about your movements being tracked, disable the GPS on your cellphone. Your phone carrier can guide you through this process.

You may wish to maintain a record of emails and texts from your soon-to-be ex, especially if there are comments relating to children's issues, or items that could be classified as abuse. Document, document, document! You can play messages into a recorder to keep them off your phone. You can send the texts to your email account and print them. Inflammatory emails should be shared with your attorney. Keep in mind that you don't have to respond to every text or message, especially when you find them upsetting. Controlling spouses may try to overwhelm you with a flurry of demands, complaints, and insults. <u>You do not need to respond.</u> Silence can send a powerful message. If the silence is too much to handle, schedule a time to answer them; let's say you'll check your texts at 11am and at 7pm. You can take control of this communication, and not let it (or your spouse) control you.

2. Open New Bank and Credit Card Accounts in Your Name

After the divorce, you'll need your own accounts and credit – but opening these accounts may be easier while you are still married. Go to a bank where you <u>don't</u> have joint accounts with your spouse, where your spouse <u>doesn't</u> have an account, and <u>not</u> where your mortgage is, and open both a savings and a checking account. You won't need a large initial deposit to open either account. You'll also need your own credit cards. Federal credit regulations and business policies can make it difficult for people with little or no income or work record to establish credit on their own. Applying while you still have joint income and assets may make getting credit easier.

If you will receive paper statements, use your new secure address. If you will use e-statements, use your new email address. Banks will require that you open your account with your legal address, and will ask for proof (driver's license, utility bills, etc.), but you can ask that an alternate mailing address be set up for all notices and statements.

3. Start Gathering Cash

Getting divorced is expensive, no matter which process you choose. In addition to ending your marital relationship, you are also unravelling an economic partnership- that is how the state views divorce. You need the best assistance you can find.

Legal, financial and counselling fees are eventually paid by the spouse who controls the funds, divided between you, or taken out of the settlement funds. You will need some money to get started. When you hire an attorney and a divorce financial advisor, they will require money paid up front, to cover the expense involved in your case. This is called a retainer. The hourly rate charged by attorneys and Certified Divorce Financial Analysts™ will vary depending upon where you live, and their expertise and experience. This is not the time to make decisions based on who is cheapest. Ask for professional referrals. Check among your friends. Most states will allow interim counsel fees to be awarded to 'level the playing field' between the spouse who controls the funds and the 'non-monied spouse', who may not have access to the marital money. This may allow you to retain a lawyer of comparable ability and reputation to your spouse's counsel, when you don't have the money on hand to pay the retainer. Your attorney should be familiar with this strategy.

Cash:

Lydia used their debit card for all grocery shopping at the supermarket and local big-box store. Short of cash, she started taking the maximum cash available, in addition to the grocery total, on every trip. After a few months, the cash began to add up, and the debit only showed as 'groceries' on the bank statement.

How much you can put aside and how easily it can be done depends on your family's financial position, and how you have managed money in the past. If you are working and have savings transferred from your paycheck, add your new account to your deductions, and either take out more, or split the deposits between the old account and the new one. That way, deposits to the existing account won't stop, but you will be saving some on the side. Drop the percentage of funds you may have deposited into your 401(k) plan until the divorce is settled, and redirect those funds into cash. (We'll talk more about 401(k)'s and other retirement accounts later). If you use ATM's, take out an extra $100 every time, and put it away. Everyone's situation is different- be as creative as you need to be.

Liquidating or transferring financial accounts before starting a divorce action is a delicate tactical decision to be discussed in advance with your attorney. You may be able to secure your half of joint funds by withdrawing them and depositing the funds into an account in your own name. The money will still have to be disclosed, but having it available can be better than having to fight over getting it back. You can also open a new account in your own name, and transfer half the investments as they are, although this may take a bit longer. It's probably not allowed after the divorce process begins. With accounts that can't be easily liquidated, you may be able to request that the bank or investment company require both of your signatures for any withdrawals. This can be useful, but is not fool-proof.

4. Document, Document, Document!

There is a lot of information that you will need, and most people don't have it all at their fingertips. It's a long list. Don't be daunted at the prospect of gathering all this information- it's not the work of one day. If you can begin this process before your divorce is legally started, it may be easier to find all the information you need. It's common, once divorce is at hand, for documents to 'disappear', statements to be redirected to another address, etc.

Betsy, unexpectedly faced with divorce, was not the 'financial' spouse, and had little knowledge of their finances. When her husband, Mike, left their home, he took not only the records, but the entire desk and file cabinet in which they had been stored! We were able to reconstruct them, but it was a long and expensive process.

Start with whatever documents you can find; the rest can be requested (sometimes formally demanded) during the divorce discovery process, if necessary. It's a long list- so I have also attached it as Appendix 1, at the end of the book.

We've said it before: marriage is about love; divorce is first about money, and second, about changing the nature of your relationship. Even if you've never been aware of it before, now you need to have a complete picture of your financial life.

So gather all the documents you can find: statements from bank and brokerage accounts, credit cards, mortgages, tax returns, W-2s, 1099's etc. Year-end statements for your investments, mortgage, pension and retirement accounts are particularly helpful, as they list all the transactions that have taken place over the entire year. Make copies of everything, and take the copies to your attorney and CDFA™. If you haven't yet built your professional team, take the documents to a trusted friend/family member, or store them in a safe deposit box that your spouse can't access- not in the trunk of your car!

You may have access online to much of this information through your financial providers and your own records, especially if you use an online service like Quicken. If not, go to your bank and ask for copies of statements, even if there is a fee for this service. One year's statements would be <u>minimum</u>; three years can be better, depending upon your situation. Even older statements can be valuable in identifying accounts and balances which may have changed over time, especially if the account is in your spouse's name alone. Credit card companies have on- line access to prior year summaries of all transactions. If both of you write checks, get copies of the checks to verify both who to whom they were payable, and who cashed them.

What She Found:

Reba went through their bank statements for the past two years, and discovered $10,000 worth of checks payable to Cash. When she got copies of the checks, she discovered that they had been cashed by Laura, who lived nearby. When she *confronted her husband, Roger, about them, he revealed that he had been paying tuition bills for Laura's daughter. Further investigation led to the disclosure that Roger and Laura had been having an affair for the past two years. Reba's portion of the settlement included an additional $5,000, in recognition of the 'wasteful dissipation' of marital funds: payable to a party unknown to the spouse, and without her consent.*

Go through your credit card statements very carefully, as you may find evidence of excessive spending, or items that you may not have shared or received (entertainment, flowers, jewelry, hotel stays, dinners, etc.). This kind of spending is called 'wasteful dissipation' of marital funds. You can often recoup a portion of these funds in your settlement.

5. Fix the House and the Car

Whether you are planning to keep the house or sell it, try to take care of outstanding maintenance and major repairs while you are still together. While this is not the time to remodel the kitchen and add a half bath, fixing the front steps, repairing that crack in the basement foundation or the leak in the bathroom ceiling are appropriate. That way, joint resources are used for the repairs, and you aren't left with important projects to do and no money to get them done. If you are considering selling the house, consult with a realtor. Get an idea of what would be needed to enhance the curb appeal and ability to sell the house and, of course, the selling price.

Get the car fixed. If you need new tires, and have been putting it off, do it now. You should also make sure there aren't any outstanding, unpaid tickets on your car, and that your registration, car insurance and driver's license are current.

Get things in order so that when you are single again, you won't have to worry about them. It's much easier to have these jobs done and paid for now, than to argue about who is responsible for them later.

6. Take Care of Necessary Medical Issues Now

While you are still together, you may have good medical insurance in place, especially if your health insurance is provided through your spouse's employer. Once you are divorced, you will not be eligible for coverage at the current rate. (See Chapter 10 for more information about insurance). If you have been putting off your annual physical, or even elective surgery, do it now.

Use it Now!

Tilda knew she would need new glasses soon. She had been having a little trouble reading small print but had put off making an appointment. She decided to see the eye doctor. Tilda got an eye check-up and two new pairs of prescription glasses while they were covered under her existing medical insurance.

7. Prepare for Future Employment

If you were planning to go back to school, especially if it will help you improve your job, or enable you to re-enter the workforce, don't put it off. If you have been out of your employment field for a while, you may need to update your certifications or licenses. Now is a good time to start thinking about what you might need to do to go back to work, or to upgrade your employment. Consider starting the education process while you have joint assets to pay for it. If you're not sure, a vocational counselor can be valuable in helping you to decide what you would like to do.

8. If You Find Yourself Under New Stress, See A Counselor For Some Help

Divorce is a very stressful time. 'Supportive therapy' can be just what you need to help you get through. Consider that helping yourself is a good way to help your children through these changes, as well.

Some states may issue an Automatic Order at the start of a divorce to maintain the 'status quo' on all family finances and responsibilities. Customary activities should continue- so start now!

9. Inventory All Your Valuables

Include items that are important to you, not only items that have resale value. Family jewelry, art, photo albums, family memorabilia, furniture handed down through the generations - things that have sentimental value.

If there are special items, including jewelry, photographs or coins that you wish to secure, do it now. Rent a safe deposit box to store them, or use that trusted friend or family member to hold them for you. You will have to declare the items and their value in your statement of net worth disclosure, but you may not have to worry about losing them in the interim.

Take photos or video of large items in-place. You may not be able to move them easily, but you will have a record of what and where they are. You should also list and photo/video items of significant value, even if you don't want to keep them.

Any items that have been inherited or gifted to you by someone other than your spouse, rightfully belong to you. Be sure to list and photograph everything you were given. If you were gifted, or inherited some things, ask the family member that handed down the item to you, or the executor, for written proof. That will make it a lot easier to ensure that they will stay with you.

Ex: Dear Becky, Enclosed is a photograph of your Grandmother Mabel, sitting on the bentwood rocker that we wanted you to have. We know that you will care for it and keep it in the family. I know that it was your mother's wish that you have her diamond ring, as well.
With love, Aunt Miranda.

Keep in mind that all property will be evaluated at its current market condition price, not at replacement value or what you paid for it. For many things, that's garage sale value. For example, although you spent $5,000 on a brand name sofa, the market value for a used sofa might be only $500.

10. Know the Status of All Property

If you will keep any big-ticket items, like a car or real estate, get all the records for those items: titles, search and survey, registrations, insurance cards, etc. If you can locate bills of sale, closing statements, records of improvements made, these will all be helpful.

11. Tax Returns

Find copies of your tax returns for the past three years. If you can't find them, verify that tax returns have been filed, and taxes paid. You can request copies of joint returns directly from the IRS, or from the tax preparer. If tax returns have not been filed, or taxes not paid, do not ignore it! The IRS has no sense of humor regarding unfiled returns and unpaid taxes. If you do not respond to notices, they can seize your property and freeze your bank accounts, even if you were not the wage-earner and had no knowledge of the tax situation. There are things that can be done to protect you. You need to see a CPA with a specialty in tax practice. Your attorney or CDFA™ should be able to recommend someone to help with this situation.

Tax returns provide a great deal of information about income of all kinds, including wages, pension benefits, dividends, capital gains and losses, business activities, as well as summaries of medical expenses, charitable gifts, etc. Your team generally asks for three years of joint tax returns.

12. Your Spouse Has the Same Rights You Do

You should be aware that your spouse is entitled to the same rights as you, for shared or joint property. Unless you have a court order stating that you have exclusive ownership of the home where you have both lived (formally called the marital residence), your spouse is entitled to access. He may legally hire a locksmith to gain entry if you have changed the locks. If you are concerned about harassment, have some cameras installed outside your home, so there will be a record of unwarranted activity. If you need to file for an order of protection to be safe in your home, do it.

He Did What???

Amanda and her husband, Adam, had a conflict-laden relationship for years. He finally moved out. Although Adam initiated the divorce, he was angry and acted out. Amanda stayed with their three small children in the marital home. During their separation, he came to the house several times in the middle of the night and dumped out her trash cans, broke the lock on her mailbox, and stole her lawn furniture. Even though she caught a glimpse of him one night, Adam denied it. This scary activity only stopped after Amanda installed motion-activated cameras around the outside of the house- and told him about them.

13. Check the Safe Deposit Box

If you already have one, visit it and check what's in there. If there are any significant assets there that you did not expect to find, it may give you a reason to start digging deeper into other places too. Inventory what you find, with a photo and a written description.

14. Social Media

Avoid the temptation to rant about your situation on your Facebook page or any other social media. Take the high road, and don't give your soon-to-be ex ammunition to use against you. Resist the temptation to blast your spouse, his attorney, the judge, etc. online. Whatever you post remains out there for all to see, and in your own words and pictures.

Posts and photos of you drinking and partying, or talking about drug use can damage your claims to be a responsible parent. Even if you don't post the picture, remember you can be tagged on someone else's page.

And- monitor, if you can, your spouse's site for exactly the same reasons.

Ron, a highly compensated professional suffering from SIDS (Sudden Income Deficiency Syndrome- more about this later) posted photos on Facebook, showing him and his paramour on expensive vacations. The posts, out of the divorce context, might have been just fun, but in the divorce setting they served to damage credibility about his lack of cash flow and claims of impending poverty.

In another case, Frank cancelled time with his son, Simon, because he "had to go to Chicago on business." Simon was suspicious, found that there was no flight scheduled to Chicago that afternoon, and checked his dad's Facebook page. There Frank was, posting about his vacation trip to Europe with his new girlfriend. She posted even more details about expensive gifts and their future plans.

15. Go Online and Get Copies of Your Credit Report

Get a copy from one of the three reporting agencies: Experian, TransUnion or Equifax. While the free credit report sites are good, they are not as complete as the 'big three'. If you have had collection activity or credit issues, I suggest you pull all three. While there is not a great deal of variance on reporting routine credit, there seems to be a larger difference between what is reported in delinquency and collection activity.

Note which credit cards and loans are open and jointly owned, and the current balances. If it is possible to get a credit report for your spouse, do so. This is a good way to determine if she has credit cards, loans, business obligations that you were not aware of. Don't be concerned if these are complicated and hard to read. Have your CDFA™ sort through the reports and your assets and debts to determine what your financial picture really looks like.

You should closely monitor credit that your spouse has access to, such as credit cards, bank loans, mortgages and home equity lines of credit. If you are concerned that your soon-to-be ex-spouse might borrow money in your name, talk to your bank about protecting yourself from future drafts against your joint home equity line of credit. You might want to sign up for a credit monitoring service, which will notify you anytime there is a change to your credit file.

If your spouse owns a business, or is a key employee, be wary of loan guarantees on business debts he may have signed, and had you sign. (For more information, see Chapter 11: Debt).

16. Stay Current on All Joint Accounts

It is very important to make payments on all credit and loan accounts on time even though you are going through a divorce. Divorce negotiations can go on for a long time. Not making payments or paying late can really hurt your credit score. Your credit rating will go down if a payment is late or missed entirely, even if your spouse is assuming the debt. Once you reach the Rebuilding phase after your divorce, your credit score may be very important, especially when you want to take out a mortgage, or buy a new or used car.

Freedom!

AnnMarie and Jim are in divorce proceedings. Jim is a business lawyer and has always handled the finances; AnnMarie has been an at-home mom for their two sons. To maintain the 'status quo', Jim deposits the required funds into their joint account, and AnnMarie uses this account for the family and her personal spending. As it is a joint account, Jim has full access to the statements. He texts AnnMarie all the time, berating her every time she spends money on herself. He criticizes her spending constantly when the children visit, telling them that their mother had better stop spending so much before he runs out of money. She's been at her wit's end, reacting to his texts and criticisms.

Finally, on advice from her CDFA™, AnnMarie went to another bank, and opened up an account in her name alone. Now she writes herself a check every month from their joint account, and deposits it into her own checking account. Jim can no longer harass her about her spending.

Talk to your attorney before taking either of these next two steps. There is strategy to divorce negotiations, even if you are not taking an adversarial path, and you want to proceed carefully.

Freeze Credit Accounts that Can't Be Closed
If you find that you are not able to close an account due to an outstanding balance, request that a freeze be placed on your account. This will prevent any further charges. You will still be jointly responsible for the balance, but no further debt can be added to the account. Remember to document all details if you do this by phone, and write and mail a letter to the credit company to confirm your instructions.

Close Joint Bank Accounts

Most couples have joint checking and savings accounts. These should be closed as soon as possible- but talk to your lawyer first. Each state has rules about withdrawing money or closing accounts once divorce proceedings start. You may continue to use your joint account, especially if your spouse is the only wage earner. If this is the case, keep your joint account open. Start a new account in your own name, and transfer funds used for your personal expenses to the new account. That way, your spouse cannot keep track of how you are spending money.

Knowledge is power; helping you to be financially empowered is our goal. Being prepared will help you achieve the best possible outcome.

For some handy checklists to help you organize your thoughts and goals, use my **Getting Started** and **Setting My Priorities** checklists.

For a free copy, go to my website:
https://www.adriennegrace.com/bonuspages/

CHAPTER 3

CHOOSING THE RIGHT DIVORCE PROCESS

What you will learn in this chapter:

Your options in choosing how to divorce:
Mediation, Collaborative practice or Litigation;
The pros and cons of each process to help you decide which one is right for you.

Well, I'm finally here. I do want a divorce, and I'm finally ready. I thought all we could do was each hire a lawyer, and then let the lawyers take care of everything. That's what my friends did, and it was awful. Now I hear that I have choices. Which way is best for me? Why is this even a financial question?

The process you choose can have a major impact on how much your divorce costs, emotionally as well as financially. I am often asked, *how much does a divorce cost? How long does it take to get divorced?*

The answer is another question: *How long will it take for you and your spouse to reach an agreement?*

How high is the level of conflict? How complex are the issues and finances involved? How well prepared are you? Who are the attorneys involved? What process have you chosen?

In addition, if you were married in a religious ceremony and may wish to remarry in the future, there are religious requirements to be considered. Each religion has its own customs and rules regarding the dissolution of a marriage, from annulment to separation to divorce. Discuss this with your clergy for the best solution. Please remember that marriage is an economic contract governed by the rules of the state where you live. A religious divorce alone will not be recognized by the civil authorities.

There are four paths you can take to achieve your divorce:
- Do-It-Yourself
- Mediation
- Collaborative Divorce
- Litigation

Here's some information to help you choose the right one for you.

Do-It-Yourself Divorce? DON'T!!!

Divorce is very complicated, in every way. As simple as it sounds, *you don't know what you don't know.* It's easy to make mistakes, and these mistakes can be irreversible and costly. There are residency rules to consider that vary state-to-state, based on where you live, not where you tied the knot. If you are in the military, there are additional considerations.

There are multiple, sworn documents to file. You need to calculate alimony. If you have children, there are co-parenting issues to work out, in addition to child support payments and shared expenses. Debts, retirement plans, pensions, investments- all have short-term and long-term consequences to consider.

Professionals work for years to master these issues, and the laws governing them are continually changing.

If you and your spouse can agree on the division of all property and all child-related matters that you are aware of, you can draft a Settlement Agreement and follow court procedures. The court of your state that has jurisdiction over divorce may be called a Family Court, Probate Court, Supreme Court or other trial Court. Many state court websites offer sample forms and even instruction booklets.

Even if you have what you feel is a simple situation, perhaps like the one above, I would still highly recommend that each of you <u>at least</u> have your own separate attorney review the final documents. You are changing your life. This is a situation that demands expertise. Don't shortchange yourself now, only to find yourself victimized by the situation later.

Do It Yourself?

Howard and Pamela are in their late 20's. They have been married just a year and a half, but have already realized that it's not working. They each work full time, and earn about the same. They don't have children, and other than student loans which they each brought into the marriage, they have no debt. They also have almost no assets, other than the furniture they bought for their new apartment. They may be able to draft their own agreement, and bring it to a Mediator or attorney to be reviewed and then filed.

There are two processes that allow you to resolve your divorce out of Court. They are referred to as Alternative Dispute Resolution methods (ADR): Mediation and Collaborative law. Each can allow you to have more control over your own divorce with the advantage of professional expertise, to avoid the expense and heartache of the adversarial process, avoid a trial in Court, and potentially save you a lot of time and money.

Mediation

In divorce Mediation, a neutral Mediator works as a facilitator. The Mediator helps both of you come to an agreement on all aspects of your separation and divorce. You are empowered to create an agreement specific to your needs. You may reach an agreement that works for you and your family but does not completely follow the case law guidelines - and that's ok.

Mediation?

Doreen and Mark have come to the end of their marriage. Although they love their two young children, they can no longer live together comfortably. Their hurt, anger, grief and guilt have cooled a bit, and they are seeing a marriage and family counselor. They can sit down and talk about how to split up without shouting at each other. Well- for a little while, at least! They want to reach an agreement that's theirs, not a judge's, and avoid heavy legal bills. Doreen suggested mediation, and Mark has agreed.

Their mediation sessions are not easy. It may be the hardest hour they have ever shared, but with the help of their Mediator, they are working through their issues, one at a time. They are beginning to realize that they are also learning how to communicate with each other in this new version of their relationship.

Your Mediator may be a lawyer, a mental health professional, or other trained individual, and must be extremely well-versed in divorce and family law. It is critical for the Mediator to be neutral and not advocate for or specifically advise either of you. *The Mediator will NOT make your decisions for you.* He will help each of you identify issues of concern, and develop options for resolving them. Mediators are neutral parties; they can help brainstorm for different solutions.

You are in the process of remaking your economic reality, so financial matters are crucial. *How can you make these critical decisions if you don't really understand your financial situation- the dollars and cents of all the bank accounts, tax impacts, investment returns, pension and retirement accounts, etc.?* Although you may be cooperating well in the Mediation, the emphasis on 'We' has turned to 'Me', and you can't rely on your soon-to-be-former partner to look out for your best interests. Often, a consultation with a specially trained financial advisor will be part of the process, to clarify these complex issues. A Certified Divorce Financial Analyst (CDFA™) has the training and skills to act as a Financial Neutral, to illuminate the financial impact of possible settlements. She can illustrate various scenarios and projections, to help both of you more clearly understand your financial options. A CDFA™ can also act as an Advocate for just you. This can be very helpful in 'leveling the playing field', particularly if you have not been active in the financial decisions of the family.

A CDFA™ can help educate the non-financial spouse to be empowered to make informed, confident decisions.

When you have come to a conclusion acceptable to both of you, the Mediator will draft your settlement agreement. This document details the terms of your divorce, division of property, custody of children, spousal maintenance/alimony, and all other issues. Non-attorney Mediators will often refer this legal task to a Mediation-friendly attorney. The Marital Settlement Agreement is a legally binding contract between you and your spouse, which goes into effect when signed, and ultimately is incorporated into a fully enforceable Court Order. The Agreement legally defines each party's rights and obligations. In many states, the Judge will review this agreement and related documents and grant your divorce without either of you actually appearing in Court.

There is just one Mediator to work with the two of you during this process. This helps your Mediation to be cost effective. A mediated divorce can often cost 50% less than an adversarial divorce, even when additional professionals have been included to illuminate specific issues.

Both of you should consider consulting separately with your own individual attorneys during the Mediation for specific legal advice (even if your Mediator is an attorney) and <u>*before*</u> signing the final agreement. Many Mediators will require this step, to help ensure that your needs have been met, all disclosures have been made, and that you have had complete legal information on which to base your decisions.

Mediators maintain their neutrality, to ensure that each of you are heard, and are not threatened or intimidated during the process. In some states, Mediation has been made a mandatory part of the divorce process. In Florida, for example, mandatory Mediation sessions can be ordered for couples who have at least one child under 18, any couple where one spouse doesn't completely agree with the terms offered by the other, and any couple with one spouse who believes the marriage could be saved. In Maryland, mandatory Mediation covers just custody and visitation issues.

If you <u>choose</u> Mediation rather than going to court, however, mandatory rules do not apply. You have the flexibility to design a plan that meets your unique needs, as long as the results are reasonable. Although case law and precedents may require a certain amount of maintenance for a specific period of time, for example, you may choose a different amount for a different period of time, as long as you both agree.

Will Mediation work for me?

If the decision to divorce was a mutual one, and you can focus on effectively ending your marriage, Mediation can be very effective. Even if the divorce was not your idea, the Mediation process has frequently been able to bring spouses to a fair and reasonable settlement. Mediation works best when there is not a super-high level of animosity or anger, or a need for revenge. If these are your issues, you may wish to add a counselor to your team, to help you work through the emotional conflict outside the Mediation process.

If you have children, another part of your divorce will be a co-parenting agreement that spells out custody, visitation and financial arrangements.

In a Mediation, you have the ability to bring in experts on various issues: a CDFA™ financial expert to explain family finances and tax issues, a business valuation expert to assess the worth of a privately held business/professional practice, or a child development expert to guide decisions regarding your co-parenting. The private nature of the process can make Mediation an ideal choice for a high net worth couple. You can avoid making sensitive financial information a matter of the public record. This is the path most often taken by many high-profile celebrities in entertainment, business, and the political world.

Mediation is about trust. If your spouse has lied to you about his behavior, you have to seriously consider if you can trust him to be honest about financial matters. If this is the case, you may not wish to rely <u>only</u> on the voluntary disclosure of information. You may ask your consulting attorney to conduct legal discovery, or at the least, require a sworn statement of net worth. Having a CDFA™ may be even more important here, to provide you with information that doesn't rely solely on your spouse's input. Trust, but verify!

In Mediation, you speak for yourself. If you have trouble standing up to your spouse in a disagreement, or if you find yourself shutting down in the face of intimidation, you may need to work with a counselor before and during the process. Or you may choose an option that provides you with more support from your lawyer.

On the 'pro' side, divorce Mediation may:
- Allow you to come to an agreement more quickly.
- Reduce expenses. It is often at least 50% less expensive than the traditional adversarial system.
- Allow for more discretion and flexibility to address personal circumstances.
- Protect privacy. Mediation is private, out of the public eye.
- Give you control over your agreement, and not leave you dependent on the discretion of a judge you can't choose and don't know .
- Result in a friendlier long-term relationship with your ex, since you address your issues yourselves, outside of court. The process may actually improve your communication skills.

- Be easier on children, since the proceedings may be more cooperative.

However, on the "con" side, divorce Mediation may:
- Waste time and money. If negotiations fail, you'll need to start over.
- Create an unfavorable outcome for you, if the Mediator is inexperienced or biased towards your spouse. Choose carefully.
- Fail to uncover certain assets. Since all financial information is voluntarily disclosed, one spouse could potentially hide assets and/or income.
- Reinforce unhealthy behavior patterns. Unless the Mediator is skilled, if one spouse is dominating and the other is submissive, the final settlement may not be fair.

Mediation can offer a less contentious, less expensive and more "respectful" way to get a divorce. If you can be reasonable and negotiate with each other, Mediation is a preferred option.

Collaborative Divorce

Collaborative Divorce is another process that allows you to work out your divorce settlement without going to court. In Collaborative law, you and your spouse have the support, guidance and protection of trained professionals who are important to all areas of your life. This is not about win-lose.

This is about win-win, with everyone focused on reaching an agreement fair to both sides.

Does an Affair Change The Divorce?

Unhappy in her marriage, Suzy found a lover, and Tom found out. The dust has settled from the big blow-out, but divorce is now declared. She knows she was wrong, but doesn't want to let her guilt dictate the terms of the divorce. Tom is a contractor, with his own successful and profitable firm.

Although he wants to press his advantage, he does not want the financial details of his company to be made public. He knows that he'll have to trade off investments and other assets, to avoid giving Suzy a piece of his business.

To be able to negotiate a fair deal on their own terms, Suzy and Tom choose collaborative practice. This way, they will be able to discuss the settlement with each other, and with their attorneys right at their sides, all the way through. They will have the benefits of an out of court settlement, without feeling too vulnerable.

Collaborative practice began in the late 1980s, with Stu Webb, who was then an experienced family law attorney, burned out on the stress of adversarial divorce practice. He became interested in Mediation and alternative dispute resolution. His vision was to bring lawyers to divorce as *problem-solvers*. Collaborative is a 'settlement only' process to help families resolve their differences creatively and respectfully, without resorting to courtroom and trial law. Starting in the United States, this movement has spread rapidly to Canada, England, Australia, Europe and Southeast Asia. More than 20 countries now offer Collaborative process as an alternative to a litigated divorce.

During a Collaborative Divorce, you and your spouse will each hire your own attorney who has been specially trained in the Collaborative process. The attorney's role in Collaborative Divorce is quite different than in a traditional divorce. Their job now is to advise and assist you in negotiating a settlement agreement out of court, and guide you in a professional and fair way. They will represent you well, but the goal of the process is an agreement, not a fight.

How does it work?

Each of you meets with your attorney separately to discuss your goals and concerns. Then, <u>with your attorney always by your side</u>, you will meet with your spouse and his attorney for all settlement discussions and negotiations. Most meetings are at least four-way, allowing you to express your concerns and negotiate face-to-face. It's really the only way in a legal proceeding that conversations can take place freely with everyone- your attorney, your spouse, her attorney and you, together.

The Collaborative process also brings in neutral professionals, as needed. A specially-trained Certified Divorce Financial Analyst™ will help both of you work through financial decisions, craft financial strategies and illuminate alternative scenarios so you can make informed financial decisions. If you have children, you will be encouraged to come to an agreement in their best interests. A neutral child development professional can be included to provide strategies to lessen the emotional damage of your separation and resolve your concerns about your kids. A coach or therapist can help keep you on track and guide you through the emotionally-charged issues that could drag out the process.

In Collaborative, you are committed to reach an agreement out of court. Therefore, you, your spouse, your attorneys and any consultants must all sign an agreement (the Participation Agreement) that requires everyone, including the lawyers and their firms, to withdraw from the case if a settlement is not reached and/or if litigation is threatened. If this happens, you must start all over again. Neither of you can use the same attorneys or consultants. This protects the confidentiality of the process, and also really emphasizes your commitment to stay out of court. This is the cornerstone of the Collaborative process: commitment to reaching an agreement out of court.

Each spouse agrees to voluntarily disclose the full details of their financial position, business assets, etc. If there is a lack of trust, or doubt about the truthfulness of these disclosures, the Collaborative process may not be right for you. With the help of your attorney, however, you may "Trust, but Verify", and request greater financial disclosure to secure your interests.

As with Mediation, when you reach agreement in the Collaborative Process, your attorney will submit the papers to enable a judge to incorporate the agreement into the Judgement/Decree of Divorce. You will usually not have to appear in court.

Although each divorce is different, many Collaborative practitioners report that it takes an average of three to five sessions to bring the matter to a close. Each of your issues can be heard and acted upon, so there is the possibility of a more cooperative relationship moving forward.

Will Collaborative Work for Me?

The Collaborative process requires substantial commitment by both of you to work effectively. Is it important to you to craft a personal solution to your divorce, rather than relying upon the decisions of a judge you cannot choose and do not know? Do you want to end your marriage with respect and integrity? Do you want to make this process easier for your children?

If you feel that coming to a reasonable division of assets, child support and maintenance agreements are more important than 'winning', then Collaborative may work for you. If reaching an equitable agreement is more important than taking revenge, then Collaborative practice may work for you. If showing your children how mature adults work together through conflict and change is important to you, then Collaborative practice may be the answer.

If you prefer to divide family assets fairly, and use your money to provide for your needs, rather than pay large litigation costs, then it may be your best solution.

DO NOT use any of these first three options – Do-It-Yourself Divorce, Mediation or Collaborative Divorce - IF:

- You suspect your spouse is lying and will continue to lie to you and hide assets/income.
- Your spouse is domineering, and you have trouble speaking up or you're afraid to voice your opinions, even with your attorney at your side.
- There is a history or threat of domestic violence (physical and/or mental) toward you and/or your children.
- You and/or your spouse have a drug or alcohol addiction, or are mentally impaired.

I Don't Know You Anymore…

Roberta and Eric had been happily married for 12 years, or so she thought. Giving up her job as a teacher to stay home after the birth of their third child was a decision of love and followed Eric's urging. After all, as an executive with a big firm, he made more than enough money to support them all, and his travel schedule was challenging to work around. Busy with children's issues, she didn't see the signals her friends later reported. Roberta felt blindsided when he abruptly declared that he was leaving her and the children. Eric moved out, declaring that he was moving in with his mother. Roberta quickly found out that instead he had purchased a condo on the other side of town. He was living with the Marketing Specialist at his firm, with whom he had been having an affair for two years. When she confronted him with this information, he cancelled the joint credit card she had always used to pay for food and the household needs, and began bombarding her with abusive text messages. Roberta felt she no longer knew the man she had married. She needed an attorney who would zealously represent her interests in a way she no longer could.

Adversarial, Litigated Divorce

When easy resolution is not possible, adversarial litigation is the solution. Even in the adversarial model, around 95% of all divorce cases do eventually reach a settlement after long and difficult negotiations, and often on the brink of a trial!

Divorce does not always involve two people mutually agreeing to end their marriage. The decision to divorce can be unilateral —one spouse wants the divorce and the other does not. Since New York became the last state to recognize "no-fault" in 2010, you don't even have to show 'grounds' for your divorce. In prior years, this might have been infidelity, abandonment, or cruel and abusive treatment. The divorce action can proceed without the consent of the other spouse. This creates an adversarial situation right from the start and often disqualifies Mediation and Collaborative, since both rely on full cooperation and voluntary disclosure of information.

An experienced divorce litigator can guide you through the process, and minimize your direct contact with your soon-to-be ex. In high conflict situations, this may be the best course of action. A good divorce attorney will help you to maintain <u>reasonable</u> expectations, and may tell you things you don't want to hear- but need to. Your attorney will prepare a clear and concise case on your behalf. You no longer have as much of a role to play in the process. Your attorney will represent you in most hearings, and communication goes between your attorney and your spouse's attorney.

Sworn statements of net worth are generally required at the start. Any documents not provided willingly can be formally demanded through the court.

Choose a specialist in family law. Case law, trends and local issues can be very important in settling your case. Ask what your attorney's approach is to settling cases: Does she have a clear game plan and a practical approach to your case? Will he stand up for your rights in the face of opposition from your spouse and spouse's attorney? You want your attorney to be a skilled negotiator. Depending on your situation, you may not want someone who is overly combative. This could prolong the pain and substantially increase your legal fees, and it may also be emotionally harmful to everyone, especially your children. Divorces can get nasty and hostile.

Even if you have tried everything else, you may still end up in court. Up until that point, both attorneys may have been "negotiators," trying to get the spouses to compromise and come to a reasonable resolution. But once in court, negotiations and compromise often take a back seat to the new goal: to "win" and get the best possible outcome for you. It will be a judge who usually knows very little about you and your family who will make the final decisions about your children, your property, your money and how you live your life. That's a very big risk for both of you to take, and that's also why the threat of going to court is usually a good motivation to reach a settlement.

If a settlement can't be reached, a trial will be scheduled. Your attorney will present your demands to the judge, backed up by your supporting documents. This can include how much money you need based upon the lifestyle previously established, the funds available to support that lifestyle, and how the assets are to be divided. There are "arguments" on both sides, i.e. reasons for the demands, presented both in writing and then orally by the attorneys representing you. Witnesses, both personal and professional (called 'expert witnesses': for example, a business valuation specialist) can be called to testify. It is not a private proceeding. It takes place in the courtroom and whoever wants to may sit in the gallery. Your attorney's focus is to present your demands as completely and favorably as possible. Your spouse's attorney will do the same. Accusations may be made, 'dirty linen' aired, family secrets bared for all to see. The judge will review all the information presented and issue a binding decision, usually within several weeks.

The judge's decision should be based on (1) The facts presented, (2) The supporting documents provided, and (3) Case law, based on other cases that have been decided over the years. Despite everyone's best efforts, there is no guarantee that the judge will decide in your favor. The judge's decision is binding and final.

This whole process can take anywhere from a year to five years or more, depending upon how contentious the issues are, how much money is involved, and how crowded the court calendar may be. It is a very expensive and emotionally taxing procedure. All communication regarding everything from taking the children on a trip to Disney, to paying the veterinarian bills, may have to go through your attorneys, who bill hourly for their time. Hourly rates for attorneys vary widely, based on where you live, and the experience, expertise and prestige of the attorney chosen. Rates can be from $250-$950 per hour. While a higher hourly rate does not guarantee a better outcome, this is not the time to shop by price alone. (More on this in Chapter 13, Building a Divorce Team). The expenses for this process are often shared between the spouses, and can come out of the money awarded in a settlement, if needed. It's an onerous process for all. With an uncooperative and combative spouse, however, it may be the only choice you have.

Here's the last piece of advice about divorce alternatives: Weigh your options carefully. Every family, and every divorce, is different. If you are able to work with your spouse to make decisions and both of you are honest and reasonable, then

Mediation or the Collaborative method may be optimal. But, if you have a complex and high conflict situation, a history of lies and evasion, or fear for your safety, a litigated divorce may be your best way to move forward.

For a helpful Process Chart illustrating the difference between these three processes, go to: https://www.adriennegrace.com/bonuspages/

CHAPTER 4

HOW MUCH WILL I NEED?

What you will learn in this chapter:

The financial side of divorce, and how to figure expenses. This chapter is about money, budgeting and the documents you will need as you begin the divorce process.
What is a Lifestyle Analysis and why do you need one?
What you think you might spend, as you establish a separate household.

We are in the process of divorce now. I never dreamed we would really end up here. My dreams are gone. What was secure and settled is now in a total uproar. I have nightmares of becoming a bag lady on the street, and my children going without. How will I get by on my own? Will I be OK?

Everyone going through a divorce wants the answer to the same question: *Will I be OK?* And the unspoken part of that question is: *How Much Money Will I Need?*

So we are here. The divorce process has started, and one of the worst parts is at hand. It's time to talk money. I know, when I say that, many of you cringe inside. Money issues come with so much baggage. Was there 'enough' in your marriage? Too little? Too much? Who controlled the finances? Who earned it? Who spent it? How much? Did you fight about it? Now is the time to face all these issues.

The first 'homework' you are likely to get from your lawyer or Mediator is contained in a thick sheaf of papers called the Financial Affidavit, Financial Statement, Affidavit of Income and Expenses, Net Worth Statement or something similar. Your attorney will likely pass it across the desk to you, ask that you complete it as soon as possible and return it to his office. You're left paging through it, with a small voice screaming inside your head: *OMG, I have no idea how to do this!*

The Financial Affidavit is basically the financial life of your marriage on paper in a formal, sworn document. It is a combination balance sheet and budget, with income and expenses, assets and liabilities, a listing of everything you own and everything you owe, and all the money you spend broken down monthly. You may have spent years avoiding this information, or you may be up-to-the-minute with it. Complex as it is, this document is perhaps the most important report of your divorce.

Your marital standard of living and your pre-divorce lifestyle are often considered as major factors in awarding maintenance/spousal support. The financial documents you create will help build your case for sufficient income for yourself and your children. Courts will use your Financial Affidavit when calculating temporary alimony and child support, and the division of property. It is critical that this information be accurate. Inaccuracies, omissions, and misstatements can damage your credibility as well as complicate negotiations about what you 'really' need. You and your spouse, who will also fill out this comprehensive report, can't "accidentally" forget about the new car he just charged on your joint credit card or the bonus you just received. Anyone who intentionally provides false information on a Financial Affidavit is committing perjury and could face serious legal action.

If you were the 'financial spouse', who paid the bills and made the investment and other decisions, this may be a bit easier. If your spouse was the financial controller (perhaps in more ways than one!), this may be more of a challenge.

Divorce is stressful to begin with and this is a big job. It's easy to end up exhausted, overwhelmed, confused and too paralyzed to do anything but guess at the numbers and leave most of the categories blank. Bad idea.

If you're feeling overwhelmed with the task of completing your Financial Affidavit, remember- you don't need to do this alone! Consult with your CDFA™, who will complete the Financial Affidavit with you/for you, as well as compile a Lifestyle Analysis. CDFA™'s are trained and experienced in dealing with these reports, and know just what's required to complete them to your best advantage, and in the least amount of time.

The Financial Affidavit is a snapshot of what you own, owe, earn and spend, now, or at the time of your separation. A Lifestyle Analysis also identifies your spending habits along with the day-to-day living expenses of the marriage, with an emphasis on the last three to five years. It's often required by the judge and serves as a verification of the net worth and income and expense statements submitted by both of you. This information is used in determining your financial settlement, and often the amount and length of time you may pay or receive alimony. The possibility of hidden assets may surface here- any large discrepancies between income and stated expenses may raise warning flags to be investigated.

Working with your CDFA™, you will get the focused attention on the accuracy and detail your Financial Affidavit needs. Your attorney will review it for general info, but has neither the time nor the inclination to go through your mortgage payments to separate out taxes from homeowner's insurance, your clothing bills from those of your children, or track individual categories unique to your household. Quite frankly, at attorney hourly rates, you don't want that, either. Your CDFA™ has the experience and expertise to move quickly through your statements, to pick up both recurring and non-recurring expenses that can make a difference to your budget- and at lower rates than your attorney.

What you really need to do is gather all the financial documents you can, both for the Financial Affidavit, and the Lifestyle Analysis. The end result will be that you have the reports properly and accurately completed. The bonus is that you will also have as clear a picture as possible of your financial situation: assets and debts that will soon be divided, and what income you need to maintain your standard of living. You'll see your spending patterns, and it's not uncommon to uncover some unexpected spending, or assets previously hidden from your view. (See Chapter 12 on Hidden Assets).

What documents are we looking for? Pretty much everything you can find: Checkbooks (or any online financial tracking program you use, like Quicken or Mint), credit card statements, bank and investment account statements. W-2's will document health insurance, retirement plans and other deductions (expenses). Credit union accounts, car loan/lease, mortgage statements and applications are important. Tax returns from current and past years, salary records, 401(k) and other benefit plan statements give needed information. Old statements may be evidence of accounts closed and transferred elsewhere. Keep the statements in a safe place and when it's time, give them all to your CDFA™. She will organize and tabulate the information for you and your attorney/Mediator. If you or your spouse are self-employed, or work with a family business, gather as much information about it as you can, including tax returns, balance sheets, loan applications, etc.

Here are some important things to consider about the budget portion of the Financial Affidavit, the expenses of your household. You can do this yourself, or use the skills of your CDFA™ to prepare it. It's important, but can be time-consuming and very confronting. Be prepared to show your expenses as they normally are. With the stress of separation, you may find that this year may not be representative of your usual spending. Maybe the family didn't take its usual long vacation, you didn't entertain as much at home, or maybe you indulged in a bit of angry shopping. Given the stress of the situation, you may have gained or lost weight, and needed some new clothes.

To give the most accurate view of your financial spending, choose a time period that better reflects your marital standard. Perhaps last year looked a little more normal than this year, and with proper documentation, you can prove the accuracy of your figures.

You Never Know...

George is a busy sales executive who travels extensively. Annette worked to maintain a stable household for their three boys. The youngest is still in college, while his brothers have recently graduated and settled on opposite ends of the country. Annette relied on George as the breadwinner. He provided handsomely for his family and insisted on taking care of all financial matters himself. Although she was well-educated and intelligent, Annette had no bank or credit accounts in her own name. She used a credit card for all household and personal shopping, and George always paid it off in full. Annette was served with divorce papers on their 20th wedding anniversary. When she stopped crying, she found that he had also stopped paying the credit card off in full, and left her with just enough credit available to retain her attorney and CDFA™ and buy a cheap bottle of wine. On instructions of her attorney, Annette gathered up credit card and bank records. Her CDFA™ prepared a lifestyle analysis that documented all activity over the last three years, enough to back up her request for temporary alimony until they can reach a divorce settlement. It also revealed thousands of dollars of jewelry and entertainment purchases that Annette had never seen.

What documents will you need? As we began to list above, basically everything that shows your financial activity, in as much detail as possible. Do you often pay in cash? Try to recall where the cash withdrawals went. To reconstruct, locate those little receipts for just about everything purchased. Try keeping a cash journal for 30 days, both to recognize your spending patterns and control cash outflow. Try posting this on a calendar, to get a better picture of how you spend cash through the month.

When doing a budget and a lifestyle analysis, gather up statements from all your bank and credit union accounts, and charge accounts, and make copies. Then write on the copy what each debit or credit charge was for. Where did the deposits come from? Get copies of cancelled checks, to verify to whom and for what they were used. Note the purpose of the payment right on the check copy.

You can set up a spreadsheet with frequently used categories (mortgage, taxes, your clothing, children's sports equipment, activities, entertainment, groceries and travel). Put in as much detail as possible. Due to the vast nature of items available at the big-box stores (Costco, BJ's, Target, Walmart, etc.) you can create a category of purchases from these stores, as 'Other'. If you can break them down further, do it. If you have pets, don't forget their expenses.

Get a copy of your mortgage application, and car loan/lease applications as well, for good information about your financial position at that time.

Get a copy of your credit report, and your spouse's also, if possible. They can be invaluable in verifying open credit accounts and other liabilities. You may even find a surprise or two here, in hidden accounts or reporting errors. Under federal law, you are entitled to a copy of your credit report, at no charge, from all three credit reporting agencies: Experian®, Equifax® and TransUnion®, once every 12 months. Your quickest option is to contact the Central Source online at www.AnnualCreditReport.com, or mail a request form to: Annual Credit Report Request Service, PO Box 105281, Atlanta, GA 30348-5281.

Business Expenses?

Scott is a part-owner and works in his thriving family business. Ruthie is a stay-at-home mom with their 16-year-old twin girls, Laura and Leeann.

Scott uses his business credit card generously. When Ruthie had their analysis done, she realized that more than $30,000 of expenses yearly were charged to his business account- including groceries, clothing, car leases, cellphones for everyone, family travel, gas and car repairs, entertainment at *restaurants, as well as food and supplies for entertaining at home.*

It was the only card they used for shopping at Costco and Sam's Club, which included a myriad of purchases for everyone in the family. That added significantly to her budget, and potentially to his income.

Things you might not think of:

- Timeshares, Country Club Memberships, Season Tickets

These can have surprisingly high value. You may wish to own these going forward or negotiate for other assets in their place. Be aware of the expenses involved in maintaining them.

- Passports

Copies of each of your passports can be useful to verify travel dates and destinations, and maybe uncover travel you may not have been aware of. If you are concerned about the safety of your minor children, be certain to collect their passports, to prevent unauthorized travel out of the United States while you and your spouse work things out.

- Medical Expenses

With the changing environment around health insurance programs, expenses this year may look very different from last year. Gather up all the Explanation of Benefits statements from your health insurer to track your co-pays and out- of- pocket medical expenses for yourself and your children, as 'Unreimbursed Medical Expenses'. If you don't have the statements, request them from your insurer. If you are not certain everything is there, contact your doctors (dentist, chiropractor, therapist, optician, allergist, etc.) for copies of your bills for the time period you are tracking. Verify copays, perhaps paid in cash. Remember to include the annual deductible as an out-of-pocket expense. If you have a high-deductible insurance plan, there may also be a Health Savings Plan to save for the co-pays, pre-tax. This is an asset which can be utilized or divided as you negotiate.

- Tax Returns

Getting the actual filed tax return from the government could provide more accurate data than your accountant's copy. For $50, payable to the IRS, you can download Form 4506 from www.IRS.gov and get copies of returns as far back as seven years. If you do have the tax returns- bring them with you when you meet with your CDFA™ and attorney.

- Tax Credits and Carryovers

If you or your spouse have had business or investment losses in previous years, they can be credited against income and lower your taxes. The loss carryover may be used annually in increments of up to $3,000 per year. A credit like this has significant value.

- Copies of Gift Tax Returns

The annual federal gift tax exclusion allows you to give away up to $15,000 (in 2019) to as many people as you wish without those gifts counting against your $11.4 million lifetime exemption. The $15,000 exclusion may be increased for inflation annually.

If you made a taxable gift (one in excess of the annual exclusion), you must file Form 709: U.S. Gift (and Generation-Skipping Transfer) Tax Return. The return is required even if you don't actually owe any gift tax because of the $11.4 million lifetime exemption (as of 2019).

- Frequent Flyer and Membership Rewards Point Balances

You may be surprised how these add up and the value they may represent in free flights, merchandise, and often cash value. They are also a clue to the volume of money which has passed through the account. Be certain to gather up, or order copies of statements on these accounts. Many credit card companies provide a year-end summary of all transactions, often categorized.

- Expenses Paid From A Business Account

These include 'perks' which pay many household expenses. You and/or your spouse may have used a company card to pay for personal expenses, which should be included in your analysis: auto leases, gasoline, car insurance, groceries, cellphones, entertainment expenses, memberships and electronics.

- Bonuses

Bonuses may be credited sporadically, or on a schedule you are not familiar with. Deferred compensation arrangements may move compensation from the year earned to a later year (often <u>after</u> the divorce).

- Employer Stock Options

These require special attention and often additional information from the employee's Human Resources Department, to properly value and consider how they may be credited, exercised and taxed.

<u>Frequently underestimated categories:</u>

- Children's Activities

Especially if your children play more than one sport, it's often surprising to add up all the costs: sports equipment, uniforms, multiple costumes, travel to tournaments, entry fees, ice time, etc., other clubs and activities, school trips, summer camp, tutoring, lessons- as well as private school tuition.

- Gifts

Active people, large extended families, busy children- it is easy to underestimate how much you spend on gifts. Make a list of all the people you buy presents for, the occasions, and how much you usually spend on the gift. Don't forget your children's teachers, service providers (hairdressers, trainers, the mailman), birthday gifts for family and for your children's friends, Christmas/Chanukah, and gifts for special occasions such as weddings, graduations, new babies, First Communion, Bar/Bat Mitzvahs. Check last year's calendar for notes on these celebrations, to estimate what gifts you gave.

- Vacation and Sick Days

Many companies allow employees to 'bank' these days if unused, and employees can receive cash payments for their value.

- Rental Fees

Expenses for storage units, docking fees for boats, seasonal storage for snowmobiles, and other 'toys' can add up fast.

Time-consuming? Absolutely. But prepared with appropriate detail, this may be your most important report in justifying a demand for support which is livable and fair, whether you are receiving or paying.

Remember, you don't need to do this alone. A Certified Divorce Financial Analyst™ (CDFA™) can help create your Financial Affidavit and Lifestyle Analysis, and, just as important, help you understand the impact of this information in building your post-divorce financial picture.

The next step is to establish a realistic budget for the future. It may be hard to acknowledge that your lifestyle and that of your children will change, but on average, household income drops by 30% post-divorce. The sooner you identify which expenses are priorities and which are optional, the easier it may be to make the transition. Consider where and how you would like to live, whether in your current home or somewhere new, and prepare a Phase 2 budget for what it will look like when you live apart. Child support is often determined by formula (See Chapter 9); focus on what you need in maintenance if there is a large difference between your spouse's and your own income. Think through what the divorce will really cost you in the long run. Inflation will become your enemy as your costs will rise; child support and maintenance are usually not adjusted for inflation or modifiable under state law, but can be by agreement.

Start to monitor your spending. Use the information from your analysis and on your calendar to catch any red flags that may appear. Unique to you and your family, things may add up annually to amounts that can surprise you. This could be anything from that daily four dollar latte, to your every-three-week manicure, season tickets to a local team or theater, spending game day at the local pub, children's treats, dining out, personal trainer, etc.

Settlement?

Ken and Layla had divorced three years ago. Ken transferred to her the money she was due from the settlement, and it was a substantial amount. He knew that she was not a good money manager, and although he had moved on, Ken still cared about her welfare. Talking with a financial advisor, he was reminded that his maintenance obligation was coming to an end in just eleven months. He texted Layla, noting that his monthly payments would stop at the end of the year. She texted back, 'Yikes!'

Things to consider when budgeting:

- Review the results of your lifestyle analysis with your CDFA™. Anticipate what you're going to spend on a monthly or annual basis. This includes the standard fixed expenses (housing costs, car payments) and variable ones (utility bills, groceries). Don't forget taxes. Don't forget those expenses that only show up quarterly or once a year, like insurance premiums, professional memberships, health clubs, and bills that are auto-debited from your accounts.
- Look at what your net income will be from work, investments and any spousal support- after tax! Child support and alimony will come to an end. Knowing when this will happen will allow you and your advisors to plan to avoid a financial crash.
- Determine whether your budget will cover a transition period. Perhaps you're going back to school or getting other career training. This is a very good conversation to have as you negotiate maintenance. An investment in your education can be productive for you and your soon-to-be ex, in enabling you to find a job, or get a better- paying one.

Education:

Josh and Darla have been in negotiations for a while. She has just been working part-time since the children were old enough to attend school, and will need to earn more to become self-supporting. Darla has been looking into a certification course in human resources management, as she used to work in that field before the kids were born. With no work experience for the past 10 years, her old certifications are all expired, and that world has changed. Josh has agreed to include the cost of her program in his maintenance payment for two years, so she can be more employable when it's complete.

For a helpful budget worksheet, go to:
https://www.adriennegrace.com/bonuspages/

See Appendix for a list of financial documents which can help you put together a complete and clear picture of your finances.

CHAPTER 5

CAN I KEEP THE HOUSE?

What you will learn in this chapter:

This is a pivotal decision- should you stay or go?
Do you want to stay?
How to determine if you can afford to stay;
Establishing the value of your house;
If you can afford to stay, what to do next;
If not, what to do next;
Refinancing /qualifying for a new mortgage;
Selling the house; other options.
There is a lot of information here. You may wish to read it through, and then come back for action items.

"I'm an excellent housekeeper. Every time I get a divorce, I keep the house." – Zsa Zsa Gabor

The House:

Jana couldn't sleep, again, as it had been the past few nights since Matt moved out. 2:30 in the morning, the house was dark and very quiet. She checked on the children; thankfully they were sound asleep. It was then that the always-nagging question came back: Should she keep the house or sell it?

She wandered through its rooms, remembering happier times- decorating Chrissy's room when she became a teenager; Matt building the racecar bed for Jack's sixth birthday; barbecues in the backyard; the fun they had designing the new kitchen, and all the mess and dust of the remodel! How to say goodbye to all that? But how to go on here without Matt? And how can she possibly pay all the bills???

For most of us, a house is more than just a box we sleep in and fill up with stuff. It's our home- the place where we create and live our lives, feel safe and raise our children. Walking from room to room can evoke years of memories, both good and bad. You may have remodeled or redecorated every inch of it, with treasured items at every turn. Yet this is a time of change. The challenge is to separate the emotional from the practical, take a long, hard look at your home, and make important decisions about it.

A house is the largest non-retirement asset most couples own together. Depending upon the housing market where you live, a house may appreciate in value over time, but still represent considerable expense and demands on your time and resources. In this chapter, we will look at what your options are, and how to make the decision which will be best for you, your family and your finances. Your house can be a refuge at a time of great change; it can be a major expense and a financial challenge; it can become a source of cash to fund a fresh start. Making that decision about the house helps to clarify other financial issues, and emotional ones, too.

As you consider the status of your home, it's also helpful to gather together all the important documents related to the property, such as the deed, mortgage or any other lien documents, the title, search and survey, documentation of major repairs, damages and improvements, and copies of any restrictive covenants which may be imposed by your community.

The first question is, 'Do I Want to Stay in this House?'

It may seem so much easier to stay than to face the reality of packing up and finding somewhere new. If you have kids, how will this next change affect them? Staying brings its own challenges, with financial demands on what may be a reduced budget, and some unhappy memories lurking around every corner. Is your house a refuge or a reminder of broken promises and unfulfilled expectations? Is staying put just a way to delay the inevitable changes, rather than face the reality of a fresh (and frightening) new start? Or is it a positive statement about where you wish to be? Do you need to divorce your house, as well as your spouse?

Change is challenging at any age. Just about all children would choose staying over moving- but this is a decision the adults must make. Many divorcing couples make the decision to keep the children in the house with a custodial parent until some future event- graduation from middle school or high school, leaving for college or graduating- and then sell. Consider all the alternatives; talk with a mental health counselor and your financial team and weigh your options before making a final decision. Now you must think clearly and be aware of financial realities that will shape your future.

Can I afford to stay in this house?

We'll get to the 'how-to' later. The next big question up front is- *If I want to, can I afford to stay in this house?* On my post-divorce income, can I pay the mortgage, taxes, utilities, repairs, maintenance and all the other expenses that we shared during the marriage?

There's not a quick answer to that question, without answering several others. We first need to know: What is the house worth? What is your equity in it?

What is the house worth?

Getting the house appraised is a good starting point, whichever strategy you choose in the end. Having a state-certified, professional appraisal done can provide an unbiased, objective valuation. A professional appraiser will look at how your house compares with sales and listings of similar homes in the area, review local price trends, and provide a multi-page written report for a fee, often in the $500-$1,000 range. To find an appraiser, ask around in your area, or go to the Appraisal Foundation website: www.appraisalfoundation.org.

No one knows your house like you do, so prepare for the appraisal. List all the special features of your home. But don't leave out the flaws. A new furnace, new windows, and whole home systems are pluses. A leaky roof, crack in the foundation and other expensive-to-fix problems are also important to mention. If your divorce is amicable, and you just need more of a guideline on your home's value, you may have a market analysis done by a real estate agent familiar with your neighborhood. The agent/broker will review recent sales and pricing, and will come to a listing price for your home, as if it would be sold. Remember that real estate agents are salespersons. Their expertise may be limited and the appraisal may be biased if the agent anticipates listing your home for sale. Typically, a written report is provided, and a fee (less than the professional appraisal) may be charged for these analyses.

Once you determine how much the house is worth, then you can figure out your equity: how much of it you really own. If you have no mortgage or home equity loan, then it's all yours. If you have a mortgage, home equity loan or a home equity line of credit, then the lender owns the house with you, and their loan has to be paid off before the house changes title.

(There are so many possibilities for exceptions, I simply suggest that you discuss this with your advisors to determine your own situation.)

Next, let's think about what repairs are needed to bring your house up to saleable condition, or to make it safe for you to live in after your divorce. If you aren't sure, you need to know what serious problems may be in place. It's a good idea to hire a home inspector to go through your house and identify potential or existing problem areas that may not have come up in the appraisal. If there is a crack in the foundation, it should be fixed before you sell. A wet basement, major plumbing, structural or heating problems should go on this list. If you can, take care of these issues now, before your divorce, while you can use joint funds to pay for them and joint resources to get them fixed. If this is not feasible, you can tally up the expenses, and suggest that this amount be deducted from the joint equity. You can then take care of them as you are able.

The Equity:

Karen and Dave jointly own their home in a pleasant suburb, with a market value of $400,000. They have a mortgage ($210,000) and a home equity line of credit they just used to pay for a new roof ($14,000). That's $400,000-$210,000 =$190,000-14,000 =$176,000.

$176,000 is the equity in their house. If they divided it equally, Karen and Dave each would be entitled to $88,000 in value.

Do this now. After the divorce, if you retain the house and find some major repair is needed, you will be solely responsible for paying for it and getting it done. If you have relied upon a 'handy' spouse to take care of repairs and regular maintenance, you may need to hire a professional in the future and pay for the work. After divorce, there may still be a 'honey-do list', but it's all yours.

If you keep the house, especially if you plan to sell it at some specified time later (for instance, when your youngest child graduates from high school), you may also agree to include closing costs as a deduction from the equity. Many areas use 5%-8% of the mortgage amount as an estimate of closing costs: Attorney fees, title search update, origination fee, credit check fee, bank appraisal, etc. There is generally no tax on the transfer of the title from joint name to yours alone while you're still married, or incident to your divorce. If you need to refinance the mortgage (we'll discuss this at greater length later), you may have many of these expenses.

Now that we know what the house is worth, and what your equity is, let's take another look at the expenses involved if you want to stay there. If you recall, we went through this information in Chapter 4: How Much Will I need?

What will it cost to live in this house?

Let's review how your living expenses add up. Are there extensive and expensive repairs required? Is the house the right size for you, as the single person or single parent you will be? Add up your income, if you are employed, any maintenance and child support that you will receive or pay, and then deduct your housing expenses- do you come out even or ahead? If so, proceed. If you can't meet the expenses of your current home on your projected income, then you need to consider selling the house or trading its equity for other marital assets and moving to a more affordable place. There is so much to consider right now; even if you plan to purchase another home, you may wish to rent for a year to give things a chance to settle down.

A Helpful Delay:

To Maggie, it seemed like the divorce took forever! Pierce was uncooperative, stubborn and made things as difficult as possible. She moved across town, to get as far away as possible from the community where they had lived together, and where he was so tightly connected. She planned to buy a house out there, as soon as the settlement money came through. She rented for a year- and then one year became two. But when the divorce was finally settled, she realized that her life took place much nearer to the community where their marital home had been. That's where her friends lived, her children and their families were, and where she belonged. So when the funds were released, Maggie bought a small house just two towns over from where her ex remained. In retrospect, she was really grateful for the delay. It helped her to make a better decision for her life after divorce.

When the answer to the question 'Can I Afford to Stay in the House?' is NO:

If the house is worth more than you owe on it, consider selling. Don't try to do it yourself. A good agent will market your home aggressively, show the house, and review potential buyers so you deal only with serious prospects.

Call the local real estate sales office, ask for the branch manager and ask who the top selling agent for your area is. This doesn't guarantee the right agent for you, but it's a good place to start. Ask friends and/or family members, and of course, ask your CDFA™ and divorce team for a referral.

Interview the agent before signing a contract. It's important to discuss how the house will be marketed, at what price, and how and when the home will be shown. Savvy real estate agents know what sells houses in the area. What changes, cosmetic or other, would make the house more desirable? And how much would they cost?

You and your soon-to-be ex must also be in agreement, as price adjustments (dropping the sale price) may be required to get the property sold in a reasonable time. You can also write in a clause in your settlement document to require an automatic decrease in the selling price if your house doesn't sell within a specified period of time.

If you are waiting for your share of the equity to be able to move on, this is a very important issue.

Always ask an agent for references. Take the time to call the former clients and ask some of the following questions:

- What did you like about selling the house through this agent? What didn't you like?
- What could the agent have done better?
- Did you get a reasonable price within a reasonable period of time?

Getting the house ready can be the most difficult part of the sale process. You **should** agree on who pays for the minor repairs, painting, etc. needed before the house is ready to be shown. If both of you have moved out by the time you put the house on the market, you can leave it to be staged by the agent. If one of you is still living there, maybe with the children, you'll need to get things cleaned up and de-cluttered. If this work falls mostly on one person, you might want to figure out a way to compensate that person for the extra effort.

When the house sells, you pay off the mortgage and home equity line of credit or home equity loan, pay the broker and closing costs, and then divide the net proceeds. You will then have cash you can use to pay off debt, find a new home, and make a fresh start.

I understand this is easier to write than it may be to read and act upon. Take a moment here, and take a deep breath. Balancing your financial stability against maintaining everyone 'in place' as your world is changing, leads to many hard choices. Determining what will be best for you and your family now and into the future requires a lot of information- and help from your team of advisors (See Chapter 13, Building a Divorce Team). A Certified Divorce Financial Analyst™ (CDFA™) can be of great assistance at this time, to help you look objectively at the finances of your situation, and help you weigh them against the emotional needs of your family.

If you are not already seeing a marriage and family therapist or counselor, please consider a consultation now. Often counselors can help you manage your feelings, and can help you help your children, as well. Your children generally feel the same feelings that you do, but lack the vocabulary to communicate them. Many counselors specialize in helping children map their way through this new landscape.

You may need to consider a different neighborhood, a new school system, and childcare and entertainment options. This is a time of change, and downsizing often means taking on many new challenges. You can do it! Luckily, children usually adapt quickly to changes in circumstances and are more resilient than you may think.

Before you proceed with listing the house, however, consider carefully where you plan to go next. If you are planning to rent for a period of time, make certain the rental cost is affordable on your new budget. If you plan to purchase a new home, review your circumstances with your team, which may now include a mortgage broker or other real estate professional. Although you may own a home jointly with your spouse now, buying a new home is really starting over. You will need to be prequalified for a mortgage for your new home, and be sure that you can borrow enough to move where you choose, based on your post-divorce income.

If you want to buy another house:

Can you afford the next house? Let's do some easy math. Carolyn wants to purchase a home for $400,000 and has a 25% down payment amount of $100,000. A mortgage of $300,000 at 4.5% with real estate taxes of $8,000 per year and insurance of $800 equals a monthly housing expense of $2,253.

Part 1: To afford this mortgage, she would need $8,046 gross income per month, or $96,552 annually, from all sources: child support, alimony, employment, retirement income, social security, and investment income.

Part 2: Carolyn's maximum allowable amount of debt payments (credit cards, car loans, student loans, and this mortgage payment) should not be greater than $2,897, or 36% of her gross monthly income. $2,253 is the mortgage part of this, so that leaves $644 for other debt payments (credit cards, car loans, student loans). If Carolyn's numbers do not fit into these parameters, it's possible that she will not be able to get a mortgage. It's far better to recognize this now than face an unpleasant surprise after her divorce is final.

What follows is a brief summary of the mortgage process. Because there are so many variables and unique circumstances, we suggest that you consult an experienced mortgage professional to help. Information on current mortgage interest rates, private mortgage insurance, credit score rehabilitation, etc. are all services that a good mortgage professional can provide to meet your specific needs. This is particularly important as the mortgage underwriting process is primarily automated. The numbers representing your income, debt, value of the house, amount you wish to borrow, your credit score- are all compiled and uploaded to "DU" or Desktop Underwriter. The DU will provide an Approve/Eligible or an

Ineligible response. All aspects of the approval are automated and the findings cannot be overturned by a real live person, so it's very important to be properly prepared.

Many banks and mortgage lenders will pre-qualify you. That is, they will let you know if you are likely to be approved for a certain amount of money before you actually make a full loan application. That way, you know what you have to work with.

The mortgage qualification process has tightened up considerably over the past several years. If you will be relying on alimony and child support to make your payments, most lenders will consider this income only when it has been documented for six months, and is documented to continue for at least three years. In most cases, a temporary order for maintenance or child support is not sufficient. The lender will require a divorce decree or property settlement/separation agreement as proof. This means it may not count until <u>after</u> your divorce is final. Be aware that you may not be able to qualify for a mortgage when you want one. You may need to rent for a period of time, or stay in your current house until such documentation can be provided.

Mortgage lenders want to be assured that you can repay the mortgage loan, so your credit score and credit history will factor into the mortgage qualification process. The amount of debt you owe, your monthly gross income post-divorce, and how much cash or equity you'll be able to use as a down payment are also factors.

The choices involved when designing a mortgage boil down to these: *How long do I want my mortgage to last? 15 years? 30 years?* The longer the term, the lower the monthly payment will be, but we need to consider how long you expect to be in the home, as well.

How much do you need to borrow? The amount of your loan, compared to the appraised value of the house, is called the loan-to-value ratio. This determines how much the lender will allow, and the interest rate you pay. Lenders want to make certain that you have sufficient commitment to the property to stay and care for it, and that you can afford to make the payments back to them. Your down payment represents your financial stake in home ownership. The higher the loan-to-value ratio, the riskier the loan is considered to be, and the higher rate you may be charged. Private mortgage insurance (PMI) is often required if you're financing more than 80% of the purchase price, and can increase your monthly costs for the life of the loan.

What is the interest rate? It will depend on your credit score, loan-to-value ratio, and prevailing interest rates at the time you apply. Do you want a fixed interest rate? Or would you prefer a variable rate loan where the interest rate often starts lower, and can adjust up or down by a set margin in response to interest rate changes?

How much is the house worth? The mortgage company will usually use its own appraisers to establish the value of the house you wish to purchase.

What are the property taxes? Depending upon the state you live in and your neighborhood, property taxes can substantially increase your monthly expenses. Don't forget to factor these in. Homeowners insurance should be in there, as well. If you are purchasing a condominium, add in those monthly fees, too.

To ensure you will have enough cash flow to make your mortgage payments, most lenders will require that the amount of your mortgage payment, principal and interest together, equals less than 28% of your gross monthly income. Your monthly debt payments, including the mortgage, taxes and insurance, are limited to less than 36% of your monthly income.

Your credit score is also part of the qualification process. In Chapter 4, we suggested that you get a copy of your credit score. This is one of the reasons why.

A lot of people who go through a divorce find it hard to stay on top of their bills. You may be experiencing delays in temporary support payments. You and your spouse may have had a misunderstanding - or a disagreement - about who will be responsible for paying which bills. If you've separated, you may already find it difficult to stretch the income that supported one household to support two; or you may have moved out and not even seen the bills. For a variety of reasons, many people find it difficult to maintain perfect credit when they go through a divorce.

Divorcing is a perfectly valid reason for late payments, as long as your credit history is usually good. But with automated underwriting, you may not get the chance to make your case. A real estate lending professional may be able to help you navigate these challenges.

If you want to keep the house, and you can afford it- how do you 'buy out' your spouse's share of the equity?

If your house is worth more than you owe, you can afford to maintain it, and you want to keep it, what's next? Given our example of Karen and Dave's $176,000 equity in their house, Karen will 'owe' Dave $88,000 for his share of the home equity, so she can 'buy out' her share. Where will she find the money?

Make the House Yours:

Karen and Dave's house is valued at $400,000, and existing mortgage and home equity balances total $224,000. Their equity is $176,000. They have divided the equity balance 50/50 as many people do, so Karen 'owes' Dave $88,000.

$400,000 value
-$224,000 loan
$176,000/2=$88,000 equity each

To make this house hers, unless she assumes the existing mortgage, she will need to borrow at least $312,000. ($210,000 refinance of the mortgage, pay off home equity line of credit $14,000 and pay off spouse $88,000). There may also be fees and taxes to be paid. These can often be included in the amount of the loan, or paid in cash.

$210,000 Mortgage
$14,000 Home Equity Loan
$88,000 Spouse equity
$312,000 Amount to borrow

Karen decides to keep the house and promises to make the mortgage payments. They leave the title in their joint names. If Karen finds she can't make the payments on time, the bank will call her for payment- and Dave, too, even though he moved out months ago.

There are basically three choices:

1. Trade-off for other assets of the marriage
2. Refinance the mortgage into your name alone, taking out sufficient cash to pay off your spouse's equity share
3. Property settlement note (often a mortgage)

Let's take these one at a time:

1. Trade-off For Other Assets

As you add up all the marital assets that will be divided, balanced against the debts, you will get a fuller picture of what there is to split. If you start from a 50/50 split (and lots of other alternatives are possible), you each are entitled to half the value of the house. In our example, that's $88,000.

You could encourage your ex to trade his $88,000 equity in the house for another asset or a combination of the items on your inventory list from Chapter 2, and your marital balance sheet from Chapter 4: savings accounts, other property, retirement accounts, investments, or even a portion of a business interest. Keep cash flow in mind when trading assets. Will you have enough income- not just numbers on the bottom line- to pay all the bills?

A classic mistake is to keep the house, and trade off all the investments and retirement accounts to balance the split. This may work for a short time. But all too often, the new sole homeowner finds that the house is too expensive to maintain on reduced post-divorce income, and has to sell to make ends meet. And often, as well, she ends up with little to no retirement funding, or cash cushion against a financial emergency. Don't let this be your story. Consult with your CDFA™, to do income and expense projections that will be helpful in managing future financial issues.

2. Refinance the House With A New Mortgage

Although you may already own the house jointly with your spouse, if you wish to take ownership into your name alone, it's like buying the house all over again.

You may need to borrow an amount sufficient to clear the existing mortgage, any other liens on the property (like a home equity loan) and to free up the cash you need to pay off your spouse's share. Then you may hold the title in just your name.

Before you make this decision, be sure that you can qualify for a mortgage big enough to cover these amounts.

See the discussion above about qualifying for a mortgage. The process is the same for refinancing.

Often you can specify in the divorce decree that the house is to be refinanced into your name alone within six months, 12 months or another time of your choosing. If this does not happen, then the house is to be sold, and the proceeds divided as you agree.

Even if your spouse is preapproved and wants to take over the property by refinancing it, we still recommend that you do not change the title on the deed until the closing of the loan, or after. Why? If you change the title to remove your name (with a quitclaim deed) and the loan does not close for whatever reason, then you remain responsible for the mortgage, but don't own the house anymore. The amount of the mortgage debt will stay on your credit report, and may prevent you from making the financial transactions you need for your own future. So wait until the refinance is complete before removing your name from the deed.

Whatever arrangements you and your spouse make regarding the division of property (including the house), if you have a mortgage, the lender is a third party to your agreement. No matter what you two decide, the mortgage company will expect to be paid. That's why it's so important to clear the existing mortgage <u>before</u> removing your name from the title.

3. A Property Settlement Note is an Alternate Way to Balance the Division of Property

A property settlement note is really a loan between the two of you. The recipient does not pay taxes on the principal -- only on the interest on the loan. The note should be collateralized; that is, there should be a tangible asset backing it up, in case your ex doesn't make the payments as agreed. For example, it could be secured by another mortgage, or you can tie it into a pension by using a Qualified Domestic Relations Order (QDRO). For more information on QDRO's, see Chapter 7: Can I Keep My Pension? Caution: Unlike alimony and child-support obligations, a property settlement note can be discharged if your ex declares bankruptcy.

House Swapping/Bird Nesting:

Robyn and Chris were married for eleven years, and have two children: Oscar is nine and Della is six. Just last year, they bought a beautiful home in a great school district, in time for Della to start kindergarten. The kids are settled into their school and doing well. Robyn and Chris are reluctant to uproot the children again so soon, on top of the emotional strain of the separation. So they have rented a two bedroom apartment close to the house. They have a detailed agreement to share space in both the apartment and their home.

Robyn will live in the house with the children for the first two weeks of the month, while Chris lives in the apartment. Chris will live in the house during the last two weeks of the month, with Robyn at the apartment. Chris pays the expenses of the house and Robyn pays for the apartment. They have each locked their bedrooms, and have a privacy agreement with an understanding not to entertain any overnight guests at the apartment. It's a challenging arrangement, but they are committed to giving their children another year in place, before reviewing other alternatives.

What if I want to sell the house, but can't?

Depending upon the housing market where you live, sometimes the home can't be sold in a reasonable amount of time – or for enough money to cover the mortgage. If the house can only be sold at a loss, there are still a few options:

1. One spouse takes the house, and rents it to the other, until the market improves enough to sell. Under these circumstances, the owner will realize any gains upon sale. This technique requires clear communication between the ex's, as you go from being joint owners to a tenant-landlord relationship on the same property.

2. Both spouses continue to own the house jointly and rent it to a third party. Again, the ex's take on a business relationship as co-owners of the property. Clear arrangements need to be made as to how the expenses of maintaining the house are to be paid, and how to share income from the rental.

3. "Bird nesting", as in the example of Robyn and Chris above, is sometimes done to provide comfort and stability for the children. The exes remain joint owners of the home. They also rent an apartment nearby, and each one alternates living in the house with the children and in the apartment on his/her own. Clear agreements are needed to provide for payment of the expenses of both residences, as well as arrangements to provide for the privacy of each ex. This is usually done for a shorter period of time, for instance, when a child will graduate from high school in six months, to allow for a smoother transition.

4. Sell the house at a loss, pay off the mortgage or other liens out of other assets, and move on.

5. Short-sale, deed in lieu of foreclosure, foreclosure, or bankruptcy.

A short sale occurs when the lender and the spouses agree to sell the house at a loss. The lender may forgive the mortgage shortage, or may require that it be paid. Although not positive, a short sale does not create the credit damage made by foreclosure or bankruptcy.

In a deed in lieu of foreclosure, the homeowners deed the house back to the lender, in exchange for the release of all obligations under the mortgage.

Deed in Lieu:

Ted and Heidi have owned a vacation condo at a favorite resort for years. Unfortunately, now that they are divorcing, property values are down. Despite everyone's best efforts, they cannot sell their condo. Too many units are for sale, and no one's buying. As a last resort, they negotiate a 'deed in lieu of foreclosure' with the bank. The bank takes ownership of the property, and has agreed to release them from the balance of the mortgage owed. This will damage their credit rating, but not as badly as foreclosure, and they get out from under an additional debt they cannot pay.

If you stop making the mortgage loan payments, the house can be subject to foreclosure. This is a lengthy legal process in which the lender can sell your property to recover the balance of the loan and the costs of collecting the debt. A foreclosure will seriously damage your credit rating, so consult your advisor team before choosing this path.

And finally, the last of last resorts, bankruptcy. Bankruptcy helps people who can no longer pay their debts get a fresh start. Their assets are liquidated to pay off their debts or they can create a repayment plan under the supervision of the court. Certain debts cannot be wiped out in bankruptcy, including alimony and child support, student loans, taxes and tax liens, condominium or co-op association fees and assessments. A bankruptcy will seriously damage your credit rating, and will remain on your credit file for seven to 10 years. Bankruptcy laws are complex. Consult your attorney and divorce team if you are contemplating this step.

Consider Irene and her husband, Edward. The couple and their children, Eddie and Danielle, lived in a beautiful neighborhood, in a $1 million-plus home. They belonged to the country club, and Irene was active in the church and community. Eddie was in high school; Danielle was in college. Negotiation resulted in alimony for 10 years, based on their 25-year marriage, with child support for Eddie till he graduated from college.

Edward paid for Eddie and Danielle's college costs. Irene received a settlement in cash, investments and retirement funds. She had no marketable career; her plans for an early and affluent retirement with her husband were gone. To shield the children from more change, and give herself time to adjust, Irene chose to stay in place. She kept their large home and comfortable lifestyle, declined vocational guidance, and dipped into the settlement funds to pay expenses when alimony was not enough.

This worked for almost seven years. The children were now out of school and on their own. When the economy took a downturn, Irene had a long-delayed meeting with her financial advisor. Her withdrawals and market declines had decreased her assets substantially. She was in danger of running out of cash, with just three years of alimony left. She finally had to face changing her lifestyle. Because she delayed so long in selling the house post-divorce, Irene had to bear all the costs of the repairs and the sale herself. Although it sold for less than she expected, the house's value had still increased dramatically since its purchase. After paying capital gains tax out of the proceeds, she had just enough left to purchase a small condo.

She began taking classes at the local community college to develop marketable skills, and found a job before maintenance ran out. Her dreams of a comfortable future were dramatically changed.

Keeping up appearances and her failure to adapt to change cost Irene **her secure and comfortable** retirement. If she had sold the house at the time of her divorce, she could have lowered her living costs, and allowed her settlement funds to grow and perhaps even generate some additional income. The costs to repair and sell their older home would have been shared with Edward, as would the capital gains tax. She might have been able to buy a modest, newer home free and clear – make a fresh start, and still have money left over for her future.

If you asked Irene how she felt about this situation, she might have different answers at different times. She might say that it was worth it- she really needed to stay and recover herself, and maintain the status quo for her children as much as she could. Or she might be regretful, not having realized the future outcome of her decision to stay, made at a time of great emotional turmoil.

You need to make the decision that's right for you. Our goal is to help make sure you are aware of the consequences of your choices, and that you can make the best-informed decision possible.

Easy-to-use worksheets are available to help you with the complex issues in this chapter:
- **Your Quick Home Inspection Checklist**
- **Repairs Needed Spreadsheet**
- **Worksheet: Can I Afford to Stay in this House?**

To request a free copy of these, go to:
https://www.adriennegrace.com/bonuspages/

CHAPTER 6

IS 50/50 FAIR? OR WHICH HALF YOU KEEP MAKES ALL THE DIFFERENCE

What you will learn in this chapter:

How to divide your property in divorce;
The difference between marital and separate property;
Identifying your priorities- what do you really want to keep?
Setting up a helpful worksheet;
Legal guidelines for community property and equitable distribution;
Tax impacts for different kinds of property and investments.

I've made a list of all of our assets, including all the stuff I want to keep, and the things I don't really care about. It's so strange to list all our things like this. There's the antique table we found at the auction, my grandmother's silver, and the rug the dog pooped on. I think I know what I want, but how do I decide what makes the most sense to keep?

Identifying and dividing assets is a crucial part of your divorce settlement. You've likely spent your marriage gathering assets and treasures of all kinds, and liabilities too: car loans, mortgages, credit cards. Perhaps you had some bank accounts, investments and student loans of your own before you married. When it comes to dividing it up, who gets what? Is it "Yours" "Mine" or "Ours"?

Keep clearly in mind that the focus shifts in divorce from "We" to "Me". Amicable or not, your spouse is no longer looking out for your best interest. You and your team need to take care of that now. Accurate information, clear documentation, and a strong divorce team are your best defenses.

And, like it or not, Uncle Sam, the tax man, can be a not-so-silent partner in the division of property and what comes next. You need to know the tax consequences of dividing and liquidating assets to be sure your result is fair and livable.

1. Dividing Property During Divorce

When thinking about dividing property, first consider your priorities.

If you don't know what you really want, you won't know what to ask for, what you may be willing to fight for, and what you can let go.

- Which assets do you really want?
- What has strong sentimental or practical value for you?
- What things are you willing to let your spouse keep?
- If something you want has a loan attached, will you have sufficient cash flow to pay the debt and the upkeep on it?
- What are the income tax consequences of your choices?
- Do either you or your spouse own or operate a business?

To decide how you will divide your property, you need to know what you have. One household will become two separate homes. What do you want in yours?

Make a list of everything of value- both sentimental and cash value. This is your property inventory.

2. What Do You List as Property?

- Real Estate: Primary home, vacation homes, rental property.
- Business owned by one or both spouses; professional practices.
    - When a business is owned, or one spouse is a part owner or key employee, it is important to get a qualified appraisal. The value of a business is often your largest asset.
- Trusts.
- Automobiles and other vehicles; classic cars.
- Recreational vehicles: snowmobiles, jet skis, boats, kayaks, RV's.
- Timeshares.
- Stocks, Bonds, Cash and Savings Accounts, Credit Union share accounts.
- Individual Retirement Accounts (Roth and Traditional), Pension Plans, 401(k)'s, 403(b)'s, 457's, Profit Sharing Plans, Deferred Compensation Plans and other funds set aside for retirement by you, and by your employer for your benefit.

- Stock options (method of determining value is complex).
- Cash value of Life Insurance Policies.
  - Term and disability insurance policies are important as well.
- Furniture and fixtures in all houses.
- Electronics: computers, video games, iPads, iPods, printers, virtual assistant (like Alexa).
- Antiques, collectibles, firearms.
- Stamps, baseball cards, sports memorabilia, music boxes, Hummels, statuary.
- Jewelry; coins, gold and other precious metals.
- Artwork; paintings, sculpture.
- Piano and other musical instruments.
- Patents, copyrights, royalties.
- Loans, mortgages, notes receivable.
- Household goods, clothing, furs, books, music, tools.
- Grills, outdoor furniture; lawn mowers, snow blowers, tractors.
- Items of sentimental value: photo albums, family memorabilia (even if they have no cash value).

The following are less common assets- but perhaps you may have some:

- Frequent flyer program miles; credit card loyalty program points.
- Commissions to be paid in the future, including trails and renewals, especially in the case of investment, insurance,

real estate professionals, consultants and attorneys. (See more about this in Chapter 12: Is Your Spouse Hiding Assets?)

- Any pending claims for damages which would impact both spouses, for example, suing a former employer for lost wages; structured and annuity settlements.
- Riparian and Mineral Rights; oil and gas leases.
- Law firm Draw Account
    - A draw account maintained by an attorney at the law firm, which is available as if it were a bank account or other cash asset.
- Foreign Asset Protection Trusts. These are usually set up in remote offshore tax and financial havens, like the Cook Islands, the Bahamas, the Caymans, Gibraltar, Mauritius, and Turks and Caicos.

Children's items are listed (Uniform Gifts to Minors and Transfer to Minors accounts, 529 plans, trusts, etc.) but may not be subject to division between parents. Be wary of these, as the parent listed as Custodian may have full authority to withdraw and move funds into and out of the account.

3. Worksheet Help

To help you get a clearer picture of where you stand, here's an easy way to set up a worksheet of your assets and priorities.

Draw four columns on a piece of paper, then follow these steps:

- Step 1. In the first column, list each major item from your Inventory.

- Step 2. In the second column, write what each thing is worth next to each description. Estimates are fine for now. If you know when a thing was purchased and what you paid for it, note it now.

- Step 3. In the third and the fourth columns, write how each item might be divided.
    - Column #3 is 'Things I want to keep'.
    - Column #4 can be headed: 'What my spouse wants to keep' or 'Things I don't want'.

- Step 4. Add up the values in each column.

Try to think about this with your head, not just your heart. The question is not only which assets you want to keep, but also which are best for your long term financial security. How do you know? Once you have made your list, discuss it with your CDFA™. She can help you review the list more objectively, and make less emotional decisions.

Adding up the values of what you want to keep, and what your spouse will have, is the beginning of your property division negotiation.

Dividing personal property is most often done between the two of you. Judges don't wish to become involved in who gets the lawn mower vs the living room sofa, and involving attorneys can add dramatically to your legal fees. Dealing with these issues between yourselves is best. If it becomes a challenging issue, consult a Mediator to help you both work it out.

In your divorce process, both of you are required to complete a sworn statement of net worth, which is also called 'financial declaration/financial statement/financial affidavit/financial disclosure', depending on where you live. You are required to fully disclose all your assets and debts. This report locks each of you into what you claim is owned. The financial disclosure also covers your budget for living expenses. (We deal with your budget and Statement of Net Worth in Chapter 4.)

4. Marital Property vs Separate Property

Remember that laws differ among states, even among states that recognize community property and the states that divide assets via equitable distribution. Consult your divorce team about specific personal issues; what follows is general information.

Property is considered in two basic categories: separate property and marital (or community) property. So, let's establish what is marital property, "Ours"; vs. separate property, "Yours or Mine".

Some Examples of Separate Property:

Paul's 401(k) plan earned before his marriage to Vera, that he rolled over into an IRA in his name. Paul has not contributed anything else to this account.

An emerald ring inherited from your Aunt Tillie.

A condo Ann owned before her marriage to Howard.

A life insurance policy your parents started for you as a child, and then signed over to you after your marriage.

The pearl necklace and earrings Nancy's parents gave her on her wedding day.

A car, titled in Margaret's name, purchased with money inherited from her grandmother.

Money awarded to Brian as damages from a car accident, kept in an account only in his name.

Money inherited from your cousin Harold, invested in an annuity in your name.

Everything you and your spouse buy or get during your marriage (before a separation agreement or the beginning of a divorce action), is considered marital, regardless of whose name it's in, or whose work or income generated it. Basically, all assets are marital, except what is designated as separate property, and that is specifically defined.

Separate property, *when kept separate*, is what each person:

- Brings into the marriage
- Inherits before and during the marriage
- Receives as a gift during the marriage from someone other than a spouse
- Receives as a personal-injury settlement (Some states have different rules; check with your attorney about specific issues)
- Has been specifically named as separate property in a written agreement, i.e. a Prenuptial or Marital Agreement

Separate property is not divided during a divorce. It's just yours.

The increase in the value of separate property is still considered separate, unless it was due to work by your spouse or the two of you during the marriage. If you mix your separate assets with marital assets, then identifying them as separate again can get complicated. You should discuss these issues with your divorce team.

Your friend, the judge?

Judy and Nathan had a stormy marriage for eight years. It finally came to an end when Judy had an affair with Aiden, Nathan's best friend from college, and Nathan found out. They tried marriage counseling to patch things up, but the sessions were filled with anger, recrimination and regret. They decided to divorce. Riddled with guilt, Judy agreed to give up everything. Tearfully, she declared, 'You can have everything! I just want out of this marriage, and to be away from you!' She moved out, and went to stay with her mother. Nathan wrote up their separation agreement, and she signed off on everything. He was the primary wage-earner, and he kept the house, his 401(k), the investment accounts, and his car. Judy kept her leased car and her personal possessions. Judy worked just part time, making minimum wage. When the settlement agreement arrived at court, the judge refused to sign it. She called them both, and demanded that they each see an attorney to review their legal rights, alimony issues, and rework the property distribution to be more equitable.

Marital Property:

While you are married, it makes no difference in whose name you buy or acquire an asset, be it an investment account, a vehicle, a house, a bracelet or a set of golf clubs. It does not matter 'whose' money or effort was used to purchase the asset, or how it is titled; it's marital.

This is a concept that some people find challenging to accept, so I'll put it several different ways. *It does not matter whose name is on the title, who made the purchase, or with what money, if you were the wage earner, or a stay at home spouse. If it was purchased or acquired during the marriage, and it's not one of the separate property exceptions, it's marital and can be divided as part of the divorce settlement.* These are all marital property if you got them from the date you married until the date a divorce complaint was filed.

Lindsey and Martin are married. These are all assets that they own as marital property:

Bank accounts, investment accounts in Lindsey's name, funded with money from her salary.

Joint checking, savings, investment accounts funded in various ways.

401(k) plan in Martin's name, based on his employment during the marriage.

Their home, in Lindsey and Martin's name jointly; down payment made from joint savings, a mortgage loan and some funds from the sale of their first home, in both names.

Vacation property in Martin's name, purchased with money he won betting on a horse.

Car titled in Lindsey's name, paid for with an auto loan in her name.

Classic 1967 Pontiac GTO that Martin bought with his annual bonus.

Graphics Design business titled in Martin's name, started during their marriage.

Pension plan benefits accrued during their marriage, from his first job, in Martin's name.

A diamond and ruby tennis bracelet that Martin gave Lindsey on the birth of their daughter, and a three-carat diamond anniversary ring he gave Lindsey on their 10th wedding anniversary.

A Rolex watch Lindsey gave to Martin on his 40th birthday.

All these are marital assets, subject to division.

When you use Mediation or Collaborative practice, you and your spouse can agree to divide your property as you see fit. If you have been informed about the law, and all assets are fully disclosed, you have more control over who gets what. This is as long as one of you doesn't give up so much of the customary property division that you might end up on public assistance.

5. Equitable Distribution vs Community Property

Equitable distribution is the division of property and debts between spouses. It can be done by agreement through a property settlement agreement, or by decree from a judge. Most states use equitable distribution to determine how a couple's assets are divided. Equitable distribution means 'fair' distribution, not automatically 50/50.

How does a court establish a fair division of marital property? How could you use these factors to make your own agreement, out of court?

Here are the factors a court will review when making the property division. It's a long list- but this is an important issue for your financial security. They vary state to state, but these are common:

- The financial condition and earning power of each spouse.
- The length of the marriage.
- The present value of all property.
- The value of each spouse's property, including a spouse's business, business interests, retirement plans, 401(k) plans, stocks, bonds, etc.
- Future financial need, debts and liabilities of each spouse.
- Probable financial future of each spouse.
- The age and health of each spouse.
- How easily the marital property could be turned into cash flow.
- Written premarital and prenuptial agreements covering property division.
- Spousal maintenance or alimony obligations to former spouses and/or children of previous relationships.
- Each spouse's income and property when they married and when they filed for divorce.
- Any award of maintenance to a spouse.
- The extent to which either spouse may have delayed pursuing education and career goals during the marriage.
- Any time and expense required for a spouse to acquire the education or training necessary to achieve a standard of living comparable to the marital standard.
- Any present or future need for medical or educational needs for either spouse or a child.

- The need of the parent with custody to live in the family home and use or own its effects (furniture, etc.).
- The pension, health insurance, and inheritance rights either spouse will lose as a result of the divorce, valued as of the date of the divorce.
- Whether either spouse has an equitable claim to marital property not titled in their name, based on that spouse's contribution of labor, money, or efforts as a spouse, parent, wage earner, or homemaker, including contributions to the other spouse's earning potential (for example, by working to put the other spouse through school).
- If the marital property includes a component or interest in a business, corporation, or profession, the difficulty of valuing that interest and whether it would be desirable for that interest to be retained intact, free from claims or interference by the other spouse.
- The tax consequences to each spouse.
- Whether either spouse has 'wastefully dissipated' marital assets.
- Whether either spouse has transferred or encumbered marital property in contemplation of divorce without fair consideration, and;
- Any other factor the court expressly finds to be a just and proper consideration.

Note that 'marital misconduct' is NOT on this list. Lying, cheating, having an affair, cutting off marital relations, refusing to communicate, ignoring your needs, not parenting your children to your expectations- are <u>not</u> factors the court is likely to consider in the division of property in most states. There are some states that will consider adultery in the ruling. As always, consult your divorce team to see what rules your state follows.

Some courts may use the division of property to penalize a spouse if he or she wasted, gambled, spent extravagantly, overused credit, spent marital money on extramarital affairs, or got rid of marital property, either during the marriage or during separation. This is called 'wasteful dissipation'. In other words, bad behavior may be relevant only if it impacts your finances.

Antiques?

Rosalee and Gary had found an antique desk at a flea market for $100. He insisted that it was an unrecognized treasure, and researched it endlessly. It went into Gary's home office. He wanted to keep it in the divorce, and noted a value for it of $100. Rosalee objected enough to have it professionally appraised.

Turns out Gary was right- it was a real antique, and worth $5,000. He can keep it- after crediting Rosalee half the appraised value, or $2,500.

Courts usually take into consideration which spouse will receive the primary responsibility of caring for their children when distributing the marital assets.

Nine states: California, Arizona, Idaho, Louisiana, Nevada, New Mexico, Texas, Washington and Wisconsin follow the community property system. Under community property, all marital property is divided equally in a divorce. Each of you has an automatic half-interest in the property and debts of the marriage, with the exception of something received from an inheritance. Whatever was acquired during the marriage with "community" money is considered to be owned equally, regardless of who purchased it.

- Assets acquired before the date of marriage or after the date of separation are not considered.
- Both the husband and wife equally own all money earned by either one of them during the marriage, even if only one spouse earns money.

In a community property state, equal ownership also applies to debts. This means both spouses are equally liable for debts, like unpaid balances on credit cards, home mortgages and car loan balances. (See Chapter 11: Debt for more information).

Realistically, however, community property does not mean that each spouse automatically gets 50% of each and every thing, but rather that the total of the assets and debts may be divided 50/50. Check with your divorce team before making any property division decisions.

Keep in mind that in a community property state, as with equitable distribution, when you use either Mediation or Collaborative process, you may agree to go outside the state formulas for the division of property. You may decide to divide things differently than a judge might. As long as you are both fully informed of your rights under the law, and the settlement is reasonable, you may do as you wish.

Stock:

Mason and Ava are divorcing and have a joint investment account, which Ava will take over. In it are 100 shares of Graggle, valued on 4/17/2017 (the date of their divorce), at $67,293. They bought it on 7/30/2010, for $24,218. The stock has gained $43,074. Good investment!

But- If Ava sells it 13 months after the divorce to help pay for her new house, the gain of $43,074 will be taxed as long term gains. In this situation, the federal income tax on her profit of $43,074 will likely be $6,461.10. The real value of this account dropped by est. 10%. (1)

6. How and When is the Value of Marital Property Established?

Marital property is usually valued when the divorce process begins. Since it can take months or years before a divorce decree becomes final, some states allow spouses to share in any change in value between the date of separation and the date of divorce.

When you can agree on the value of assets and property, the court will generally accept what you decide. When you can't agree, you have to give the court evidence or proof, like bills of sale, receipts, and business records. On some items, like artwork, collectibles and antiques, expert testimony may be needed to establish value. A professional appraisal can be used to value real estate and other items.

It's important that you understand both the distribution laws of your state, as well as the decisions of the family law courts in your area, especially if you are going to litigate. This is where your divorce team will be very helpful.

7. Tax Issues – Why 50/50 May Not Be Fair

The IRS gave up trying to tax transfers of property between husbands and wives long ago- too hard to track, too much trouble. However, after divorce, when you may need to sell some securities to raise money for your new house, or you find that the only available cash is in a retirement account, taxes will become an additional expense and the inequity of your settlement may become distressingly clear.

A little background here. Don't worry, I'll keep it simple. The Cost Basis for an investment is usually the purchase price, adjusted for stock splits, dividends and capital distributions. You use this number to figure the profit or loss on an investment, and for tax purposes. When you receive an investment account transferred from your spouse in the divorce, the value of the account shows as of that day. When you receive the stock or mutual fund, the original cost basis is transferred as well. The increase in value is considered to be a capital gain, and capital gains are taxable income. Short term gains, when you sell within a year of its purchase, are taxed at your regular income tax rate. Long term gains, if you hold the stock a year or more before selling it, are taxed at a lower rate.

Wouldn't you want to know about the tax consequences of your choices before you finish negotiating the exchange of assets in your settlement?

Good news. Most investment companies will track your basis right on the statement, so you can see 'unrealized gain or loss'. Unrealized means it's not taxable yet, but will be when you sell it. So before you agree to accept one asset or another, check its after-tax value, not just what shows on the Statement of Net Worth.

There can be taxes due when you sell the house and when you withdraw money from retirement accounts, as well. Be informed and be prepared. (For more information about the tax consequences of selling retirement investments, see Chapter 7: Can I Keep My Pension?)

8. Will You Have Enough Cash?

When dividing your assets and debts, don't forget to consider your cash flow, or spendable income. It's great to have a big number on your balance sheet, but if you can't pay your bills without selling something (and paying tax and penalties), then it's not the best deal. Financial professionals call this Liquidity. It's your ability to convert an asset into cash- money in your pocket, or in your checking account. A money market account can be turned into cash quickly; a mutual fund can usually be turned into cash in three to five days; a classic car, however, is not a source of ready cash. All too often, one spouse will end up with mostly illiquid assets that do not generate income, like the house, while the other takes liquid assets which generate interest, dividends and capital gains, like brokerage and retirement accounts.

If you plan to take most of your value in your home, make sure you have enough cash flow to handle the bills, not just now, but down the road as well. If not, then you may find you have to sell your house, downsize, or reduce expenses in ways that may not be comfortable, as a result of an unworkable settlement.

Be sure to check out all these options with your attorney, CDFA™, and accountant. These decisions involve complex concepts and laws, and you want to get it right the first time. They can help to ensure that your settlement is fair and reasonable and help you to move on to financial independence.

(1) *Assuming the price of the stock is unchanged. Ava has $100,000 of ordinary income, with no deductions, and files single. In 2019, her federal income tax would be est. $18,174.50. Federal income tax on the long-term gain of $43,074 at a 15% rate, would add an additional $646.10 tax due. State income tax may also be due. And, if Ava had higher income, she could potentially owe an additional 3.8% tax on net investment income, and Alternative Minimum Tax.*

To get a helpful worksheet, **Dividing Assets**, visit **https://www.adriennegrace.com/bonuspages/**.

CHAPTER 7

CAN I KEEP MY PENSION?

What you will learn in this chapter:

What are retirement accounts;
How to put a value on a pension;
How to value and divide 401(k) and IRA plans;
Taxes and penalties possible upon withdrawal from retirement funds;
How to make an informed decision about keeping or giving up retirement assets.

"I'll do what's fair", Penny said. "I'll keep the house, and you can keep your pension and retirement plan. After all, you earned it, while I stayed home with the kids."

This may be what you say- but deep down, are you harboring the fear of being a bag lady in your old age? Are you concerned that you'll have to work forever? Financial security is a major worry for most couples. Retirement funds, in all their formats, are an important part of that long-term security. Giving them up, or sharing them, can generate fear in even the most stable of financial partners.

So let's take another look at this emotional choice, provide some more information and then see what decision you'd make.

Retirement accounts and pension plans can represent a major part of your net worth. While you were married, the two of you likely saved and dreamed of your retirement together. You may have concentrated your savings into just the accounts of the higher-earning spouse, or tried to save in each of your names. It doesn't matter. All these accounts are marital property to be divided the same way as other investments. Pensions, retirement accounts (IRA, Roth IRA, SEP IRA, SIMPLE IRA) and employer-sponsored plans: 401(k), 403(b), 457 plans, deferred compensation, employee stock options and ownership, profit sharing and other similar plans are all included. The amount you can divide begins to accumulate on the day you are married and generally stops the day you file for divorce.

Feelings of ownership regarding the retirement funds often come up, especially if responsibilities were divided in your marriage with one spouse staying home with the family and the other building a career outside. He may think, "I earned this; I worked long hours (and still do!), endured an unpleasant boss, and paid all the bills. Why should I share the benefits?" You may even agree. But recognize, as the law does, that whether you worked outside the home or spent your day as a homemaker, your duties have value. You are part of the economic partnership that was your marriage and all benefits that accrued are marital property.

1. Defined Benefit (pensions) and Defined Contribution Plans

Most retirement accounts are funded by pre-tax contributions made from your wages and processed through payroll deduction by your employer. Your contribution is fixed as a percentage of salary, with maximum limits established every year. Some employers will make an extra contribution to employee accounts, and may also match a percentage of the contribution. You, as the employee, make the choice of how the money is invested, based on the investments available in the plan. The amount of future retirement income depends on how much you have contributed and the investment performance over time. These accounts are called Defined Contribution plans.

On the other hand, pension plan benefits are a function of how many years you've been on the job and how much you've earned. Pension plans are funded by your employer, and are designed to provide a fixed amount of lifetime income upon retirement. Pensions pay a specific dollar amount every month, based on a formula. The formula includes the average of your last few years' salary, a set percentage of benefit, and how many years you worked. These plans are called Defined Benefit plans.

Pension Math:

Kevin has just celebrated his 20th anniversary working for DEF Inc. His wife, Kitty, helped him get the job. He never dreamed he'd stay there for 20 years! He can't wait to take his pension and retire. The average of his last four years' salary is $97,500. Using his company's formula for pension benefits: $97,500 x 2.15% x 20 years= $41,925, or $3,193.75 per month. This is Kevin's guaranteed income for his lifetime. Since he was married for the entire time he worked at DEF, his pension is a marital asset.

If either of you had one of these plans before you married, it's considered your separate property, and not divided. If you were married part or all of the time you were covered by these plans, there is a specific formula used to determine the percentage of marital vs separate property. In New York, the formula is named for, and based on, a divorce case for a couple named Majauskas. This formula provides an ex-spouse with one-half of that part of the Participant's pension earned during the marriage. Your CDFA™ can calculate this for you, as well as estimate the value of that pension's lifetime benefit in today's dollars. This can help you to make a more informed decision about what to choose. 50/50 is the most frequent split, but it's not the only option. Sometimes there is an unequal division, or a trade-off against another asset (like your house).

All retirement funds that qualify as marital property can be divided, but how you do it depends upon a number of factors.

Federal guidelines under the Employee Retirement Income Security Act of 1974 (ERISA) control the division of funds in 401(k), 403(b), pensions and other similar plans. State laws dictate how all types of IRAs (Individual Retirement Accounts), SEP's (Simplified Employee Pension Plans) and SIMPLE IRAs (Savings Incentive Match Plan for Employees) are divided. It's critical that your divorce settlement agreement clearly spells out how the assets are split and how those funds will be transferred. Military pensions and federal, state, county, city, town and firefighter retirement plans all have their own rules regarding division during divorce, and some will not make direct payments to former spouses.

Pension Math (2):

Peter and Penny have been married for 20 years. He is 55 years old. Peter has a pension from PPY, Inc., which will pay him $4,000 a month for life, if he works there until he retires at age 65. He has worked for PPY since he and Penny were married. Based on these assumptions, the total value of his pension is $561,510- the value today, of the future flow of monthly income over Peter's lifetime. The marital share (based on the total time Peter works at PPY vs the total time he was married) is valued at $380,704, almost 68% of the total. If they split this amount 50/50, Penny's share would be worth $190,352. The balance, based on the time Peter works after the divorce, is $180,806- this is Peter's separate part. Penny may not be able to get her share paid out in a lump sum, or get to it until Peter is 65; her share would be lifetime income for Penny, as well. She could take this future benefit as part of her retirement plan, or recognize the current value, and trade it off for another asset. If Peter does not continue to work for PPY, he may not qualify for his full pension. Peter and Penny both share that risk.

When you recognize that the pension benefit is worth over $190,000- might that change your initial reaction to not consider it?

2. Dividing Retirement Plans

Plans covered by ERISA require a Qualified Domestic Relations Order (QDRO) issued and signed by the judge, to give the administrator instructions on how to divide the money. A QDRO allows the funds in a retirement account to be separated into two different accounts- one for the employee and the other for the non-employee spouse. The money in the non-employee's account can be left there, withdrawn, or rolled over into a retirement account (typically your own IRA). Most people choose to roll it over into their own accounts, under their own control.

Don't make the mistake of assuming that just the divorce settlement agreement will protect your share of the retirement account. You need a properly prepared QDRO, usually done by specialist attorneys. Payment of their fee should be negotiated between the spouses. It is recommended to obtain a "pre-approval" of a QDRO to avoid unpleasant mistakes well before your divorce is finalized.

3. Making Withdrawals from Retirement Plans

IRA, 401(k), and other retirement plans were designed to help you save for retirement by giving a tax deduction when you contribute, so income taxes are due when funds are withdrawn. Designed to be used for retirement income, a 10% additional tax penalty is charged on withdrawals made from your plan when you are under 59½ years old. There are a few exceptions for IRA's, but divorce is not one of them. Roth IRA contributions do not enjoy a tax deduction; only the gains on the contributions are taxed and penalized at early withdrawal (before age 59½ and if the account has not been open for five-plus years). Plans covered by ERISA have an additional loophole. While it's not good financial planning to use retirement money for any other purpose, when it's the only money available, you can get to it.

Under section (72(t)(2)(c) of the Internal Revenue Code, the non-employee spouse can make a withdrawal from a Qualified Plan, such as a 401(k), without the 10% penalty, even if they are under age 59½. To avoid the penalty in the case of a divorce, you must comply with all three of the following:

1. The retirement plan must be a qualified plan covered by ERISA (e.g. 401(k) and other retirement plans).
2. The funds must be paid to the nonemployee spouse.
3. A Qualified Domestic Relations Order (QDRO) must be submitted to divide the plan.

The amount paid out from the retirement plan as cash is taxable income. The custodian of the plan is required to withhold 20% of the distribution to prepay the tax. So if you need the money for bills or other expenses, consider that the amount you get will be 80% of what you take out. Money rolled over to your IRA from your spouse's 401(k) is not taxed at transfer, but only when you withdraw it.

401(k) Math:

Desmond and Patty are divorcing. As part of the settlement agreement, Patty is awarded 50% of Desmond's $300,000 401(k), or $150,000. She needs $40,000 to pay her attorney and some other bills. Her attorney drafts a QDRO that directs Desmond's employer to transfer 50% of the plan funds to Patty. Once that's done, Patty requests a withdrawal of $50,000. Penny receives $40,000 in a check, with $10,000 (20% of the amount withdrawn) withheld to prepay the federal income tax. When she files her tax return, that $50,000 will be taxable income. At a 25% tax rate, Patty may have to pay $12,500 in federal tax, making her $50,000 withdrawal more like $37,500 (less state tax, too!).

$150,000 = $300,000 x 50%
 -50,000 withdrawal to pay bills
$100,000 available for rollover

$50,000 withdrawal
-10,000 withheld for tax
$40,000 proceeds

-2,500 additional tax payable
$37,500 net proceeds

Then Patty has the remaining $100,000 transferred to her own IRA, nontaxable until it's withdrawn. There is no IRS penalty for this transfer. If Patty did not need the cash, she could just transfer the full amount from Desmond's 401(k) to her own IRA, and pay no income tax on the entire $150,000, until she withdraws it.

A QDRO is not necessary to divide any of the types of IRA's; a letter of instruction from the owner, a distribution form, and a copy of the divorce settlement document will usually be sufficient. But be careful. If, instead of ordering a transfer to your spouse's IRA from yours, you just withdraw the money from your IRA and then write your ex a check, the IRS treats that like a regular withdrawal. If you're under 59½, that would trigger income tax and a 10% penalty on the withdrawal - and your ex doesn't have to pay any of the tax or penalty.

Consult your CDFA™ and/or your CPA to make sure you get what you need, and avoid taxation and penalties whenever possible.

There are more issues than you might think, even when you agree to divide your retirement plans 50/50. Suppose you agree that your spouse gets half of your IRA, valued at $300,000 as of the settlement date. The divorce order then says he should get $150,000. If the market crashes and your account value drops to $200,000 - suddenly he is getting 75%

of the total. Vague language, like 'divide retirement benefits in half' isn't good either. Most retirement accounts are invested in mutual funds, whose value fluctuates. You want to be sure that market gains and losses, based on the values as of the dates you agree on, are factored in.

4. Questions to Ask

Here are some questions to ask and things to consider when your agreement is being drafted:

A. What is the valuation date to be used to determine your share in the retirement plan? Is it date of filing or date of separation? This can create an issue, especially when the participant is still working and contributing.

B. You also want to make certain that the employee does not withdraw from the funds while you are negotiating about them. This should be a clear agreement when you start this process.

C. Does the plan include some separate property? Make sure you have the value as of the date of marriage, and as of the date of separation or filing.

D. Should you agree to a specific dollar amount now or when the plan is divided? State whether investment gains/losses should be included.

E. How is the money currently invested? The investment style will impact how the account performs over time, and impact the amount of market risk the funds are exposed to.

F. Find out the amounts of any withdrawals, distributions or loans to the participant during your marriage. If there is an outstanding loan, you need to determine whether the loan value should be included in the total. What was the money used for?

G. Have you factored in the taxes due on withdrawal, either now or in the future?

If you are in the military, or married to an active duty serviceperson or veteran, there are several unique characteristics to retirement and other benefits in divorce. Be sure your team has expertise in military divorce matters.

Avoid this Tax Mistake!

In Donald and Maria's divorce settlement, Donald gets 50% of Maria's $300,000 IRA. He needs the money to pay off marital credit cards, so instead of directing her IRA Custodian to transfer that amount to his IRA, Maria makes the withdrawal herself. She writes him a check for $150,000.

The following year, Maria is appalled when she goes to file her income tax return and finds that she has to pay tax on the full $150,000 plus an additional 10% penalty (she is 57 years old). What does this mean? Let's estimate the impact. Let's assume no deductions, she files Single in 2019, and makes $70,000 per year. Normally, her marginal tax rate would be 22% and she would pay approx. $11,259 in federal income tax. (She may have state tax to pay as well). Given the withdrawal from her IRA for Donald, her taxable income just jumped up to $220,000: $70,000 + $150,000. Her marginal tax rate has bounced up to

35% and her tax due would be est. $52,194+ $15,000 (the 10% penalty) = $67,194. OMG!

5. Additional Information

You may be eligible for Social Security benefits, as the divorced spouse of a worker who qualifies, even if you have never worked yourself. This is a benefit available to you through the Social Security Administration, not the court, not through a negotiation or divorce settlement. You do not need your ex's permission to apply, nor does he/she even have to be aware of it. Your benefit does <u>not</u> impact the amount of your spouse's benefit. All you need is your ex's social security number, date of birth, and proof of your marriage and divorce.

To be eligible, your marriage has to have lasted 10 years or longer. If you are considering divorce and you're not quite at 10 years yet, it may be worth it to delay until you have reached this important anniversary.

You may collect Social Security benefits on your ex's work record if:

- You are not married;
- You are age 62 or older;
- Your ex-spouse worked for at least 10 years and paid into the Social Security system, and is entitled to Social Security retirement or disability benefits.

Social Security Solution:

Debbie and Rich were married for eleven years when they were young, and then divorced. Rich remarried, and went on to a successful, well-paid career. Debbie never remarried, and worked as a freelance photographer. She had a good professional life, but never made much money.

When retirement came around, she was worried that she wouldn't be able to get by. She talked to her advisor and was relieved when she found that she was eligible for Social Security on Rich's account- and the amount would be equal to half the amount Rich would be eligible to receive! That's a lot more than she earned on her own. Debbie carried no ill-will against Rich and was grateful to realize that her benefit would not diminish his in any way. And, a bit embarrassed, was also grateful that he didn't have to know about her claiming benefits on his account.

If you are eligible for retirement benefits on your own record, Social Security will pay that amount first. But if half of the benefit on his/her record is more than yours, you may get a combination of benefits that equals that higher amount (reduced for age, if either of you is younger than full retirement age).

There is a lot more information available. Please visit www.socialsecurity.gov for more details.

You decide how much of the retirement benefits of your marriage you wish to keep. But make your decision with all the information at hand, so you can be confident that it's in your best interest both now and in the future.

CHAPTER 8

ALIMONY

What you will learn in this chapter:

**Types of alimony/separate maintenance/spousal support/ spousal maintenance/ (all terms used interchangeably);
Factors involved in calculating who pays, how much and for how long.**

"Whew! I'm sure I'll get alimony since he makes so much more than me. That will make my life so much easier. With the child support, I'll be able to stay home with the children, keep the house, and everything will be just like it was before"...she fantasized.

There's nothing new about the concept of alimony. The word itself comes from the Latin word *alimonia*, meaning nourishment, sustenance.

Alimony is mentioned as far back as in the Code of Hammurabi (1754 BC) and the Justinian Code (AD 529-565). Laws and Courts have never been favorable to wives, although back then, *if* a husband was convicted of murder, *if* he consorted with prostitutes in the family home, or *if* he whipped his wife, then she could end the marriage and recover her dowry. United States law is based on English common law, back to a time when a woman's property was transferred to her husband upon her marriage. When the marriage ended, he kept his wife's property and in exchange, was obligated to provide for her.

Now, alimony is money paid by one spouse to the other after a divorce. It's structured by a written agreement or court order, to allow the recipient to maintain the lifestyle enjoyed during the marriage, as closely as possible on the given resources. "The Duchess should not be required to live on the wages of the scullery maid" after a divorce. *Casper v. Casper*, 510 S.W.2d 253 (1974 Ky.) The terms maintenance, spousal/separate maintenance, and spousal support are often used interchangeably with alimony, and we will, too. Please note- I said <u>Recipient</u>, not Wife. The law is gender neutral; husbands can receive alimony as well as wives.

The saying goes: 'Two can live as cheaply as one', but the reverse is certainly not true. The income that supported one household will now have to cover two separate homes. While maintaining the standard of living of your marriage is the goal, it is not always achievable. After a divorce, estimates of household income drop about 23-40% for women. (1) 'Gray divorce', divorce for spouses over 50 years old, can be financially catastrophic, particularly for women who have been out of the labor force and are closer to retirement age.

The harsher impact for women is often because raising children is expensive and time consuming, and mothers are still most often the primary child care providers and custodial parents. According to a 2011 report derived from the U.S.

Census, 56.6% of custodial parents did not receive the full child support awarded. Even with joint custody agreements, only 43.7% of child support is fully paid, and the issue of how much is paid on time is not addressed. (2)

The 'gender gap' is another factor. A study by the American Association of University Women, Spring, 2016, (3) says that, on average, a white, non-Hispanic woman who worked full time all year made <u>78 cents for each dollar</u> earned by a man working similar hours. If that woman is black, she made <u>63 cents for each dollar</u> earned by a white man. If she is Hispanic, she made <u>54 cents for every dollar</u> a white male earned. Women, out of the workforce for years, caring for children and maintaining the household while their husbands have been advancing their careers, are at greater disadvantage. And the pay gap grows with age.

Spousal support can help bridge the gap. When do you qualify for alimony? Generally, it's paid when there is a difference between your income and earning capacity vs your ex's. Spousal maintenance was designed to help support the lower-earning spouse, or one who has been out of the workforce, to transition into becoming self-supporting. The basis for awarding maintenance is not for the punishment of a guilty spouse but rather to continue to support the other. Whichever of you earns more, may be required to pay alimony to the other. It is not gender specific. Women who are the higher earners in their marriages may have to pay alimony to their husbands.

The payment of alimony is an important divorce financial planning and negotiating tool. Until December 31, 2018, alimony negotiations came with tax issues. Alimony was deductible to the spouse who paid it and became taxable income to the recipient. It was a way to provide a tax break to the higher income payer - and shift the tax burden to the spouse who was usually in a lower tax bracket. If your settlement was negotiated and final by December 31, 2018, then this tax status will hold for you, for the length of your alimony. For divorces finalized in 2019 and forward, alimony is tax-neutral as to federal income tax. This means there is no longer a tax deduction to the payer. No federal income tax will be payable on alimony received.

As of January, 2019, not all of the states have clarified their positions on the taxability of alimony. As happens in so many divorce-related issues, rules may differ state-to-state. Please check with your local counsel to be certain you are clear on how your settlement will be treated. It will be tax-neutral on your federal return, but might retain tax-deductible/taxable status on your state tax return.

Child support is unchanged, tax-neutral with no tax issues to either party. It's considered to be funds paid by the parents for the benefit of the children.

Compromises were often made between the two payments, to allow for tax benefits that made the overall package more attractive to a higher-income payer. This is no longer an option. Both alimony and child support are paid with after-tax dollars with no special treatment by the IRS.

The laws governing spousal support vary state to state. There is no set formula across the board, although several states have them, at least for temporary maintenance (pendente lite). If you and your spouse can reach a reasonable agreement on the terms – the amount of maintenance needed, and for how long it will be paid, the court will generally approve it. If you can't reach an agreement, the judge will decide for you, often after a costly trial to determine and rule on the facts of your case as presented, and the guidelines for your area.

Given the changes in our society, the trend has been to award spousal support less often, and to shorten the period it's paid (called 'duration'). If your incomes are close to the same, and both of you are employed, there may be none. The larger the difference in income earning or potential, and the longer the marriage lasted, the longer spousal support may be paid- even for life. Maintenance ends as specified in the agreement, or when either the payer or recipient dies, and often when the recipient remarries, or lives with a new partner.

Maintenance is paid in addition to the assets you keep as a part of equitable distribution or community property, although the income-producing potential of these assets is counted in figuring the amount due. Before you start negotiating with your spouse about alimony, consider what judges look at when awarding spousal support.

Here is the California statute, for example.

In ordering spousal support under this part, the court shall consider all of the following circumstances:

(a) The extent to which the earning capacity of each party is sufficient to maintain the standard of living established during the marriage, taking into account all of the following:

(1) The marketable skills of the supported party; the job market for those skills; the time and expenses required for the supported party to acquire the appropriate education or training to develop those skills; and the possible need for retraining or education to acquire other, more marketable skills or employment.

(2) The extent to which the supported party's present or future earning capacity is impaired by periods of unemployment that were incurred during the marriage to permit the supported party to devote time to domestic duties.

(b) The extent to which the supported party contributed to the attainment of an education, training, a career position, or a license by the supporting party.

(c) The ability of the supporting party to pay spousal support, taking into account the supporting party's earning capacity, earned and unearned income, assets, and standard of living.

(d) The needs of each party based on the standard of living established during the marriage.

(e) The obligations and assets, including the separate property, of each party.

(f) The duration of the marriage.

(g) The ability of the supported party to engage in gainful employment without unduly interfering with the interests of dependent children in the custody of the party.

(h) The age and health of the parties.

(i) Documented evidence of any history of domestic violence, as defined in Section 6211, between the parties, including, but not limited to, consideration of emotional distress resulting from domestic violence perpetrated against the supported party by the supporting party, and consideration of any history of violence against the supporting party by the supported party.

(j) The immediate and specific tax consequences to each party.

(k) The balance of the hardships to each party.

(l) The goal that the supported party shall be self-supporting within a reasonable period of time. Except in the case of a marriage of long duration as described in Section 4336, a "reasonable period of time" for purposes of this section generally shall be one-half the length of the marriage. However, nothing in this section is intended to limit the court's discretion to order support for a greater or lesser length of time, based on any of the other factors listed in this section, Section 4336, and the circumstances of the parties.

(m) The criminal conviction of an abusive spouse shall be considered in making a reduction or elimination of a spousal support award.

(n) Any other factors the court determines are just and equitable. (California Code - Sections: 4320, 4324, 4330)

Alimony:

Sylvia and Bernie were married for 18 years. This was Sylvia's second marriage; she is 10 years older than Bernie. When they married, he was just finishing law school, and she was a nurse. He graduated, and over the years, became a very successful, very highly paid attorney. After their daughter was born, Sylvia was severely injured while lifting a patient.

In addition, she developed severe arthritis, and was declared fully disabled by the Department of Social Services. She can take care of Anna, their daughter, but can't work outside the home. In their divorce, while the guidelines suggest 30-40% the length of the marriage, or 5.4-7.2 years for the duration of alimony, she was awarded alimony for 20 years.

Few states specifically list domestic violence in awarding maintenance.

Additionally, if you have special needs, these would be considered, such as:

- A serious medical condition which requires on-going medical treatment.
- A learning or other disability.
- An issue for which you are receiving therapy, counseling or psychological care.

If this is the case, it is likely that your attorney will need a copy of the medical records from your doctor, psychologist, therapist or other provider to back up your claims.

Some states allow courts to consider marital fault (bad behavior) in determining whether and how much maintenance should be granted. Georgia will not award alimony to a spouse guilty of desertion or adultery; North Carolina, Florida, Pennsylvania, Alabama, Idaho and Mississippi will consider any marital misconduct in awarding maintenance. Minnesota will specifically not consider marital misconduct.

Texas has the most restrictive rules: The Texas court cannot order maintenance for more than three years unless there are physical or mental disabilities in the spouse which prevents him/her from earning a living, or a child of the marriage has such a disability. The Texas court must limit the maintenance to the shortest reasonable time period that allows the recipient to earn an income and care for his or her minimal requirements. And - the Texas Family Code limits the amount a court can order for alimony to the lesser of $2,500 or 20 percent of the spouse's average monthly gross income- no matter the standard of living of the marriage.

Plan Ahead:

MaryBeth and Jason had three small children at the time of their divorce. Luke and Liam were two years old, and Gabriella was six. MaryBeth was an elementary school teacher for five years before she became pregnant with Gaby, but has not worked since then. Jason, a doctor with a growing practice, felt she should be at home and MaryBeth gladly agreed. She is now the custodial parent, since Jason moved out to be with his new girlfriend. They were married for eight years.

MaryBeth needs child support to pay for the children's needs; she needs spousal support to be able to stay home and care for them at least until the boys are in school. They may be delayed for a year, to allow their speech skills to improve before starting kindergarten. The guidelines would award maintenance for just over three years, but Jason and MaryBeth have agreed on maintenance for over four years, until the boys are in kindergarten. After that, MaryBeth will need to be ready to re-enter the workforce. College courses, new requirements for teacher certification- she needs to map out what to do to be ready for fulltime work at that time, or before. And how much it will cost, so arrangements can be made to provide those funds

Most bad behavior: lying, cheating, having an affair, not listening, being irresponsible, not meeting your needs or not being there for the children are not usually factors for awarding alimony. Do not expect the judge to consider these in calculating how much you will receive, unless this behavior resulted in economic damage to the marriage. 'Wasteful dissipation' of assets refers to wasting marital funds by extravagant spending, gambling, overuse of credit cards, speculative stock trading, and funding extramarital affairs, etc. Mississippi, Ohio, Maine and New Jersey will specifically consider dissipation of assets in awarding maintenance.

Whether you're the one who'll be receiving or paying support, you need information to negotiate effectively. Otherwise, how could you feel comfortable that the support you agree to is adequate for your needs—or consistent with your ability to pay? Before proceeding further, feel free to go back to Chapter 4: How Much Will I need? Consult with your CDFA™ to help you work out this crucial issue.

Types of Alimony

There are a number of different types of alimony with different purposes. Be sure to consult with your divorce team to determine the rules in your area.

1. Temporary Spousal Support/Alimony:

Also referred to as "pendente lite," temporary spousal support is money paid while you are separated, to allow the other spouse to maintain the family's lifestyle between separation and divorce. You can either agree on a reasonable amount, or it can be awarded via a temporary court order. Although it's called temporary, it may last months or years, until your divorce is final. Don't rely on the judge's estimation of your needs; rarely does this work in the recipient's favor.

If you go to trial, the court will use your budget, among other factors, in determining the appropriate amount of maintenance. The amount awarded for temporary maintenance is often made permanent, so figure carefully! If you are using Mediation or Collaborative process, the same information will be needed to allow you to calculate your needs, or ability to pay. It's important that your monthly living expenses be as comprehensive yet realistic as possible, as they may be challenged during intense negotiations. You may want to refer to your Certified Divorce Financial Analyst™ for the lifestyle analysis discussed in Chapter 4, to ensure an accurate calculation of your needs.

2. Rehabilitative alimony:

This is designed to provide time and money for the disadvantaged spouse to pursue education or job training to become self-sufficient and financially independent. It's also given to the parent of small children so she may care for them at home until they reach school age. It is usually paid for a short-fixed period of time. If you are the receiving spouse, you will want to make sure that your final divorce settlement includes a clause allowing for a review of spousal support after the term. This means that you may ask the court to review your case at the end of your fixed time, and determine if spousal support should be continued, or the amount changed.

3. Reimbursement Spousal Support/Alimony:

Reimbursement Spousal Support is paid so that one spouse can "reimburse" the other for certain expenses, often used in short-term marriage. For example, if during your marriage you worked to help put your spouse through dental school, you may be able to get spousal support to recoup the money you spent to help fund his education and build his career. The payments can be made in a lump sum or over a period of time. Remarriage does not terminate the reimbursement support obligation.

4. Permanent alimony:

Permanent maintenance is paid to one spouse for life. It ends only when the payer dies, or at the death or remarriage of the recipient. It is rarely awarded unless there is a serious medical issue, in the case of very long term marriage, or with an older partner. If you are receiving permanent spousal support, it's a good idea to ensure that your spouse carries a life insurance policy naming you as the beneficiary. That way, if he dies before you, your support will not die with him. (See Chapter 10: Guaranteeing Child Support and Alimony for more information about this.) Permanent spousal support can be reviewed and modified to reflect a change in circumstances for either of you.

If you want to modify your order for spousal support, you must show the court that financial circumstances have changed for you as the payer or as the recipient.

Commonly accepted reasons for modification are:

- Three years since the agreement was signed **and**
- 15% involuntary increase or decrease in either party's income or
- Substantial change of circumstances

5. Lump-sum alimony, or alimony buy-out:

Sometimes, it can be better for you to do an immediate buy-out of spousal maintenance- a financial settlement right now-

and be done. You agree to a lump sum up-front, rather than having your ex pay alimony to you monthly.

No More Arguing:

Angelina and Ben have been married for 16 years. It has been a volatile relationship, and that has led to a contentious divorce. They have each rejected several proposals made by the other, and finally reached a settlement agreement, literally on the eve of a trial. Angelina just knows that Ben will continue to fight her.

Rather than fight for each payment, she will take a lump-sum settlement instead. They have sufficient money for Ben to be able to pay it up front, as calculated by her CDFA™ and confirmed by his CPA.

Angelina will take this lump sum of money and invest it carefully to provide her own income stream. Then she will never have to argue with Ben over payments.

The amount and length of time are fixed by contract, even if it is paid over years. No modifications can be ordered, no matter if the ex passes away, or the recipient remarries or lives with a new partner. This method of maintenance provides the cleanest break. There is no longer a financial link; the ex's need have nothing further to do with each other, unless there are children involved. The recipient has the freedom to spend and invest the funds as she wishes, to provide for her needs. If the plan doesn't work out well, there is no recourse.

When would it make sense to consider an alternative to regular, monthly maintenance payments from your ex?

1. When relations have deteriorated to the point of discomfort, and you can't rely on his conforming to even a court order without a fight.
2. When her income is variable, such as on commission or bonus, and production can vary widely from year-to-year.
3. When there are sufficient assets on hand now, which may not remain.

Discuss this option carefully with your attorney and CDFA™, and your CPA to determine the tax and other consequences of this arrangement.

Be as sure as you can that your settlement is something you can live with for at least the term of your spousal support, and that the payer will have future income to sustain it. Don't hold out for promises you know your spouse can't or won't keep. If your ex does not abide by the terms of your agreement, the enforcement of spousal support payments can lead you back to court, with substantial expense in time and money. This can happen even in collaborative or mediated settlements, although you're more likely to go back to mediate rather than sue in court. Your settlement needs to be workable, and reasonable for both of you. Most maintenance awards do not have inflation clauses, so look toward the end of your support term- and plan for the future. When alimony is short term, take advantage of the time to prepare to become self-supporting. Take classes, renew certifications, consult a vocational counselor to help figure out what kind of work suits you best. Don't allow yourself to be caught unprepared when your maintenance comes to an end and your income drops dramatically. Your CDFA™ can be very helpful in mapping income projections and working with you to develop your post-divorce budget and future financial plan.

Identify your priorities at the outset. Once you sign the agreement, anything not in it won't be included. Negotiate for possible future events and contingencies- even death and disability. (For more information on this issue, see Chapter 10).

Be sure to consult an attorney to review your agreement BEFORE you sign it, even in Mediation. Consult with your own mediation-friendly attorney, to review the agreement. That way, you can make sure that all your rights are protected, you understand all that is in it, and the agreement is the best it can be. Your professionals work with divorce all the time. Most couples divorce only once and simply don't have the experience and knowledge to handle all the issues effectively. *You don't know what you don't know!*

Once your agreement is signed, make the most of this time to develop your skills and empower yourself for the next stage of your life.

(1) The cost of breaking up - Institute for Research on Poverty, *Laura Tach and Alicia Eads* University of Wisconsin-Madison
(2) Custodial Mothers and Fathers and Their Child Support: 2011 Current Population Reports by Timothy Grall, Issued October

2013 P60-246. U.S. Department of Commerce Economics and Statistics Administration U.S. CENSUS BUREAU census.gov

(3) The Simple Truth About the Gender Pay Gap, Spring 2016 edition, American Association of University Women

CHAPTER 9

CHILD SUPPORT

What you will learn in this chapter:

Child custody;
How to estimate the amount of child support;
Future issues: how to pay for college.

I am so concerned about the kids. All the disruption, disagreements, drama at home, and then Ian moving out- the children are taking this badly. Jimmie has become very quiet, and won't talk about anything anymore. Janis Is acting out and refuses to talk to her father when he calls. And I'm even more worried about Kurt, who acts like nothing has changed. How do we continue to parent them, as separate people? And how do I pay all their bills, on my little salary?

When children are involved, often a co-parenting agreement is established before discussing child support amounts. You set out the very real issues of visitation, access, time-sharing and agreements about the care of your children. This can cover real time parenting issues. Will the children have overnights and weekends with each parent? Where will your son spend his birthday? Summer vacation? Who will take your daughter to early morning practices? It involves building a schedule that the parents can live with, and which will give the children some continuity, a new normal to live in, and an agreement to cover their special expenses.

There are two kinds of custody: legal custody and physical custody. Physical custody, also known as primary residential custody, sets where the child will live most of the time, usually with one parent. Legal custody gives the both parents the right to make major decisions about the child's welfare, up to age 18 or 21. Often one parent will have physical custody, while sharing joint legal custody with the other parent. The noncustodial parent is generally required to pay child support, and visitation is arranged to suit the parents' schedules and the children's needs.

There are as many variations on this as there are different parents and children. Alternative arrangements are frequently made to suit individual circumstances.

The amount of child support paid is based on the income of both parents, the number of children, the expenses of the custodial parent, and any special needs of the child. In many states or counties, a chart is provided online that factors in all this information. Check to see if your locality posts this information on its website. It may also include health insurance coverage, school tuition or other expenses. Child support continues by law until:

- the child reaches an emancipation age of 18 or 21;

- by agreement- often defined as graduation from high school or college;
- at a specified age, like 22 or 23;
- or the child is otherwise emancipated. A child can be considered emancipated (no longer under the control or the responsibility of the parents) when he's 18 to 21 years old (depends on the state and his student status), or if she marries, enlists in the military or is removed from disability status by a court order.

As with spousal maintenance, in New York, the amount of child support can be modified by a court order, if a change of circumstance relating to the parents or the child is proven:

- Substantial unanticipated change in circumstances,
- Three years have passed,
- And a 15-plus percent change in income of either parent.

Child support is separate from spousal maintenance. Child support is not tax-deductible by the payer and not taxed as income to the recipient. It's just considered to be carrying out the duties of parents to support their children. In New York, the motto is "Every Child Has The Right to Support from Both Parents".

Child support is calculated by estimating the amount of support that would have been available to the children if the marriage had not failed, depending on the combined income of the parents and the number of children involved. A percentage of family income, often up to a certain 'cap' set by the state, is used to calculate the amounts due.

In Ohio, they normally cap income at $150,000 but can use actual income when crafting a child support order. In Nebraska, the amount 'normally' considered is $120,000 net income, with deviation considered when income is greater.

In New York, Child Support Percentages are:

One Child 17%
Two Children 25%
Three Children 29%
Four Children 31%
Five-plus Children no less than 35%

The earnings considered include just about everything: workers compensation, disability payments, unemployment and retirement benefits, salary and rental income, commissions, bonuses, and many other forms of income. In calculating income, any amount paid for spousal maintenance is deducted from the payer's income, and added to the recipient's income <u>before</u> doing the child support calculation. Required basic support usually is increased to cover children's health care expenses not covered by insurance, and reasonable child care expenses if the custodial parent is working, in school, or in a vocational training program. Also considered are special or enhanced educational expenses of the children.

In many states, the court can use its discretion to determine the presumptively correct amount of child support, at variance with all charts and formulas, on a case-by-case basis.

A support order will be issued by the court.

The support of a child is held in high regard in our society. A person who fails to pay ordered child support can be held in contempt of court. States have different ways to act against parents who don't pay what they owe. These measures are often wide-ranging and highly focused on enforcement. In New York, the Child Support Enforcement Units and Support Collection Units will enforce the order automatically through income withholding and, where appropriate, collect unpaid support by collecting tax refunds and lottery winnings, seizing bank accounts, suspending driver's licenses, suspending or denying passports, and notifying credit reporting agencies of past due child support. The case can be sent for collection to the state Department of Taxation and Finance. If that's not successful, an enforcement petition can be filed with the court. The court can then:

- order money judgments;
- order hearings to suspend state-issued business, professional, recreational or occupational licenses;
- issue probation or jail sentences;
- or refer the noncustodial parent to work or rehabilitation programs.

In negotiations, Mediation or Collaborative, you may set your own amount and add-ons, as long as the court would not find them "unconscionable". Normally, the payer of child support makes payments directly to the recipient, or to a specified service provider (like a school), or it can be done through the state child support agency or support enforcement unit.

The settlement agreement spells out the terms and conditions dealing with medical insurance coverage for the child and the payment of medical bills. Childcare is an add-on expense.

Deviation Factors

If the court finds its guidelines unjust for a particular case, considerations for adjustments may include:

- Special or unusual needs of the child;
- Obligations for other minor or handicapped children;
- Other court-ordered payments;
- Extended visitation or extraordinary expenses for visitation;
- Mandatory wage deductions;
- A great difference in income in the two parents' households;
- Benefits that either parent receives from remarrying or from sharing living expenses with others;
- Taxes;
- Significant contributions from a parent toward the child's expenses;
- The financial resources and earning power of the child;

- The standard of living of each parent and the standard of living the child would have enjoyed if the marriage had continued;
- The age and the physical, emotional and general needs of the child;
- The medical and educational needs of the child;
- Comparing the earning power, financial resources, assets, needs and obligations of each parent;
- The educational aptitude of the child and any educational opportunities;
- The responsibility of each parent for the support of others;
- The value of services contributed by the custodial parent;
- Other relevant factors.

Private school tuition, for instance, is a deviation factor.

College Planning

Hannah and Alvin have been divorced for just two years. Their daughter, Erin, is now ready for college. Hannah and Erin have done the college tour and have identified a 'safety' school, a top choice, and a back-up. As the custodial parent, Hannah will fill out the FAFSA, based on her lower income. They are hoping for a generous financial aid package which will allow Erin to go to her first choice school. Alvin and Hannah will then divide the balance of her school expenses based on their relative incomes. Alvin will pay 75% and Hannah will take care of the remaining 25%, as they had agreed two years ago.

If you have children and dream of their college graduation, you may want to include an agreement about how each parent will contribute to college expenses. This may be very long-range planning for you, especially if your kids are still small. Considering the long-term impact of inflation, education costs are likely to be very significant. You can agree to share the cost of post-secondary education (two-year, four-year college or university, or vocational school) at a certain percentage (50/50, 60/40, or in proportion to your incomes at the time, called pro-rata). Often parents will specify that they will pay up to the amount that a public college education would cost at that time, after applying available grants, scholarships, and financial aid. If your child wants to go to a more expensive private school, your ex won't be bound to pay the difference, but might do it anyway.

With young children, you could also postpone the conversation, and agree to review your financials in the two years before your kids are ready for college.

If college is closer, you can include in your agreement that the lower-earning parent takes care of applying for all available financial aid and filing the FAFSA (Free Application for Federal Student Aid).

As you can see- there's a lot to consider! That's why you need your divorce team to help guide you to make the best settlement agreement possible, for now, and later as well.

For additional help in working out college expenses, go to: https://www.adriennegrace.com/going-from-we-to-me-bonus-pages/, for the **College Student Budget Worksheet**.

CHAPTER 10

INSURANCE: GUARANTEEING CHILD SUPPORT AND ALIMONY

What you will learn in this chapter:

How to secure child support and alimony payments with insurance;
How to structure a life insurance policy to meet your needs;
Protecting against disability;
Health insurance;
Long-term care insurance.

We have a pretty comprehensive agreement. Whew! There are a lot of numbers in here, over a lot of years. The kids are small, so they'll need that child support for 12-15 years. And I'll need that alimony to transition back into the working world. What if something happens to their father? What if he died? Or got sick and couldn't work? What would I do??

As you, your divorce team, and your soon-to-be ex negotiate your settlement, you are likely to find there are a lot of long-term promises built in. Child support will usually last until your children are 18, or 21, or graduate from college, or a related later age like 22 or 23. Maintenance can last just a few years or much longer, depending on the length of your marriage. Your future may be riding on the continuing earning power of your spouse. What if he died unexpectedly, or she became disabled and unable to earn her usual income- and unable to pay you? How do you protect yourself and your children? Sustainable settlement terms, careful wording of your settlement document, and insurance can help you do this. We've discussed how to reach a reasonable and workable settlement in previous chapters. Let's focus on your protection tools now.

Life Insurance

Life insurance is an amazing tool, and it's designed to do just what you need when an ex-spouse/parent passes away. Life insurance provides the cash to fulfill the obligations of the settlement: a lump sum of money to pay the mortgage, and/or at least some of the children's education/ living expenses. You can spend or invest that lump sum, or turn it into a stream of income for life. You usually include in your agreement the stipulation that the supporting spouse maintains an existing life insurance policy or gets one. Life insurance proceeds (the death benefit) are paid directly to the named beneficiary upon proof of death and the claim documents. Life insurance passes outside your will; you don't need to go to court to collect it. Insurance proceeds are also income tax-free.

How much do you need? For how long? A Certified Divorce Financial Analyst™ can help you figure out how much: the value today of the sum of the monthly payments you are counting on, over the time period you agree to. So the insurance would need to be in place from the time of your divorce until the term of your alimony has ended, or your children have reached the age specified in the settlement.

Insurance Needs

Caitlin and Patrick are divorcing. Patrick is liable for child support payments of $1,000 per month until 10-year old Chad turns 21. The sum total at stake is approx. $132,000. Patrick has a life insurance policy in force now, with a death benefit of $250,000, with Caitlin as beneficiary.

Cheryl is 53 and her ex, Charlie, has agreed to maintenance payments of $100,000 per year until she turns 65. Cheryl needs to protect a benefit of approx. $1,200,000. Charlie's life insurance in force only has a death benefit of $750,000. Additional life insurance is needed, if he can qualify for it.

The amount needed is figured using the 'discounted present value'. This is based on the concept that the value <u>today</u> of a stream of cash payments, or a future sum of money, is less than it will be if it earned interest over that time period. Discuss this with your divorce team.

Child support and spousal support obligations end at the death of the person who's paying it (the payer), so an untimely end can create a major financial hardship for you as the recipient. There are some other alternatives to cover child support at the death of a parent: Social Security survivor benefits payable until a child is 18; a claim can be placed against the estate (if adequate funds are available); or even a Qualified Domestic

Relations Order (QDRO) could be used to tap into retirement funds, if there are any.

For spousal support, you may place a claim against your ex's estate, and often such a provision has been written into the agreement, but there is no guarantee that the funds will be there for you. Social Security survivor benefits are available for a divorced spouse but are limited.

Life insurance that pays out the amount you have agreed to upon the death of your ex is the guarantee you need.

Here's a little information about life insurance:

A life insurance policy involves four components: the company that issues the policy (the issuer), the owner, the insured and the beneficiary.

1. **The issuer** is the insurance company. You want a company that is financially healthy, to deliver on the future promise. Check out its rating, provided by several private companies that do financial analysis of insurance companies. Ratings of A's and B's denote financially strong insurers. There are a lot of other factors to consider, so get assistance from a qualified insurance professional, who can provide you with policy recommendations based on ratings, and also on experience with the recommended companies.

2. **The owner** of the policy pays the premiums and controls it: the amount of the death benefit, loans against any cash

value, if the policy even stays in force, and who is the beneficiary.

3. **The insured** is the person whose life is covered by the policy. On the insured's death, the death benefit of the policy is paid by the insurance company to the designated beneficiary.

4. **The beneficiary** is the person or entity (trust, estate) who gets the benefit when the insured passes away. A contingent beneficiary gets the death benefit if the primary beneficiary has died first.

You can be the insured, and also own the policy. Of course, you can't be the insured and the beneficiary at the same time! But when the policy is covering your ex, guaranteeing child support and alimony payments, we recommend that you, as the recipient and/or custodial parent, either own the policy and be the beneficiary, or be named the irrevocable beneficiary.

Why? If your ex-spouse owned the policy, she could simply stop making the premium payments and let the coverage lapse, or change the named beneficiary to a new love interest.

Imagine the consequences if you relied on the policy benefits and they were not there! As the owner, you are notified of any outstanding issues, like non-payment of the premium, and can prevent the policy from lapsing or being cancelled. Proof of insurance should be required on an annual basis, just to be sure. If you are not the owner and do not control the policy, you can include a stipulation in the settlement agreement that if the beneficiary is changed or if the policy lapses, you or your children would be entitled to a portion of your ex's estate equal in value to the death benefit. However, insurance death claims are usually paid very quickly; court processes to claim against an estate have very long timelines, indeed.

If a new policy is needed, your soon-to-be-ex must agree; you can't get a life insurance policy without the insured's knowledge and consent. Depending upon the amount of coverage you need, your ex may have to take a physical exam and provide some medical information. If she has health issues, including a history of depression, coverage may be hard to obtain. Consult with your CDFA™ or a life insurance professional for guidance as to what coverage may be possible, and the cost. The proposed insured should go through the underwriting process prior to signing the settlement agreement. If coverage will not be available due to health issues, or if the premiums are too expensive, other provisions should be included in the settlement to protect against your financial loss, as outlined above.

Insurance Benefits

Hillary and Barney were finally at the end of their long negotiation, and even longer separation. They had finally agreed upon the terms of the divorce, and signed the papers. There were not a lot of marital assets; they had moved around a lot, following Barney's career. The settlement and spousal *support meant a lot to Hillary; she really needed some time to rebuild her skills, now that she would be out on her own. Her team had done their due diligence, making sure, among other things, that Hillary remained as beneficiary on his life insurance policies, totaling $750,000.*

Five days later, the team got a phone call from deeply distressed Hillary. Barney had gone out with his friends to celebrate the divorce, had a few beers too many, and crashed his motorcycle. He was dead on the scene. When Hillary was able to deal with business again, she realized that her financial future was now secure. A very mixed blessing.

Who pays the premiums?

If your ex pays the cost of the premiums, unless otherwise agreed, the amount can be included in alimony payments. If you pay them yourself, you can include the premium cost in your living expenses- the cost of peace of mind.

To protect your maintenance payments, you should be named as beneficiary, with your children or a Trust for them as contingent beneficiary. This will make sure that if you should die first, the insurance benefit will go to the kids, not to anyone else. To secure child support, should the beneficiary be the custodial parent, a designated custodian, a trust for the benefit of the children, or an Irrevocable Life Insurance Trust (ILIT)? There are advantages and disadvantages to each. Be aware that placing the proceeds in a custodian account, or naming minor children as beneficiaries, will eventually give 18 year-olds access to a substantial sum of cash, unsupervised. Discuss this issue with your divorce team before naming your beneficiary on either an existing or a new policy.

Although the amount of insurance needed to cover your benefit will decrease every year, the death benefit of the insurance policies may not be as flexible. Some types of insurance will allow you to decrease the benefit amount, but most policies, especially term life, will not. If insurance needs will continue for a long period of time, you can purchase several smaller term policies, with different maturity dates. Or, you may use a policy with a long term, and simply stop paying the premiums when the time required has passed.

What type of insurance do you buy?

The most popular types of life insurance products are level term, universal life, and whole life insurance.

Level Term life insurance has premiums that stay the same every year, and a guaranteed death benefit for a specified period of time. If the insured dies within that time, the death benefit is paid. If she survives the policy, no benefit is due. Term insurance is also often available on a group basis, through employment or professional associations. It's usually the lowest-cost option. Most insurance companies issue policies for 10 year, 20 year and 30 year terms.

A **whole life policy** has guaranteed premiums which will remain level for the insured's entire life, and cash value that grows every year.

Universal life is a type of flexible permanent life insurance, with the low-cost protection of term life insurance as well as a savings component invested to provide cash value buildup.

Variable universal life insurance is a type of flexible permanent life insurance, which provides a death benefit with the option to accumulate cash value by choosing from a variety of investment options included in the policy. Cash values will vary, depending upon the performance of the investment options selected, and are not guaranteed.

Consult your CDFA™ or a life insurance professional to determine the best solution for your particular needs and resources. If either of you owns a life insurance policy before the divorce is completed, consider these options before deciding what to do with the policy.

Permanent insurance may have value beyond the cash surrender value and the death benefit you see on the statement. Some life insurance policies can be traded online, or sold to a third party. Consult with your team and a life insurance professional for more information on this strategy. In certain circumstances, this may also apply to Term Insurance, even though it usually has no cash value.

Whole life insurance policies are desirable assets. They pay dividends and the cash value that accumulates is tax deferred. So the 'living' value of a whole life policy can grow in a way that is not dependent upon the stock market. Usually, the person who's insured keeps the life insurance policy and pays half the cash value to their spouse. Since the policy has some unique and desirable features, consider keeping it for yourself. Ownership of an existing policy can be transferred to the spouse who wants to maintain it. You can own the policy whether or not you are the insured.

Before liquidating a cash value life insurance policy, consider a 1035 exchange. This allows the owner of the policy to 'rollover' the cash value of the insurance into an annuity- without any immediate income tax due. The annuity can then provide income for the recipient. Income tax is due when income is received, which may be at a later date. This can be an attractive alternative to paying tax on the liquidation of an insurance policy, and losing its future value.

Disability Income Insurance

Disability income insurance may be your next-most important long term guarantee of maintenance and child support. People under age 65 are three times more likely to become disabled than to die. If your alimony-paying ex becomes disabled, this is classically a 'change in circumstances'. This can trigger an adjustment in support payments- at a time when the disabled person may be unable to deal with the demands and stress of filing for relief. And you as the recipient spouse still need the income!

Disability Insurance is the plan that provides for periodic payments of benefits if you're unable to work due to a sickness or injury. It can help meet expenses and maintain your standard of living by replacing anywhere from 45% to 70% of gross employment income, often on a tax-free basis. Disability insurance is available through employer-sponsored programs, or on an individual basis. The insurance company will set the maximum monthly benefit based on occupation and income.

That kind of policy is designed to pay the minimum living expenses of the insured, while disabled. It's not really structured to meet alimony and child support payments, as well.

There is a divorce settlement disability policy that's specifically designed to pay most or all of the expenses stipulated in the divorce decree. This can include spousal support, child support, children's medical insurance premiums, private school and college expenses, etc., if the payer becomes disabled - not limited to a percentage of gross income. The premiums for coverage are surprisingly low, considering the sum total of benefits. Check with your CDFA™ and divorce team for more information about policies like this.

Finally, as you adapt to your new single status, don't forget to evaluate your own insurance coverage—- for both disability and death. Make sure your children don't end up paying the price if something unexpected happens to you.

Disability

Jennifer and Paul enjoyed a very affluent lifestyle during their marriage. He was very highly compensated, and the family, with two active young children, lived up to that standard. When divorce came, there were a lot of assets in the settlement, and a high alimony payment. The children attended private schools, and were active in several expensive sports. Both Jennifer and Paul planned for them to attend private universities, and that's all in the agreement. To make sure that these future obligations are funded, Paul has adequate life insurance. But in case Paul becomes ill or disabled and can't work, they want to make sure the cash flow is funded, as well.

They purchased a disability insurance policy which covers his entire obligation: spousal maintenance, tuition for the children's current schools, sports activities, as well as future college expenses. Jennifer pays the premium with dollars included in her spousal support. She can be confident that the children's lifestyle- and hers, too- will be protected.

Health Insurance

Many couples share health insurance under one of their employee benefits packages during the marriage; while you may maintain coverage during a separation, you may not continue sharing coverage once you are divorced.

While employed, you may be able to get health insurance from your own plan after your divorce. Or you can remain on your spouse's group policy, keeping the same coverage for up to 36 months. You pay the full cost of coverage (without the employer's subsidy), plus an additional charge for administration, under the federal law known as the Consolidated Omnibus Budget Reconciliation Act, or COBRA. This can often be the most expensive option.

The Affordable Care Act (ACA) has made major changes to health insurance. The ACA requires insurance companies to have plans to cover people who don't have health insurance available at work, or are not employed, or who have existing health conditions. The state insurance 'marketplaces' created by the ACA offer health insurance options when you don't have access through your employer. Buying insurance through your state's marketplace may cost less than paying for COBRA coverage.

Health insurance is a major expense, whichever program you choose. In addition to the premiums, most insurance programs include co-pays for many services, as well as high deductible amounts. Deductibles represent the amount you need to pay out-of-pocket before the insurance begins to pay for your treatments, and can be thousands of dollars for many plans. Spouses who are not employed should carefully investigate future health insurance costs, and be sure to include them in your budget. As with most issues, check with your divorce team to determine your state's regulation.

You also need to determine which parent will provide your children's health insurance coverage, and how the differential between single and family coverage will be paid. Sharing payment of uninsured health care costs, like copays, costs for medical, dental, eye care, psychotherapy, etc. will also need to be decided.

Long-term Care Insurance

With more people 50-plus divorcing, long-term care issues become more important. You may have planned on caring for your spouse, or having your spouse care for you, when you became elderly, frail, or ill. That may no longer be an option. Long-term care insurance can help you pay for the care you need, whether you are living at home, in an assisted living facility, or a nursing home. The insurance might also pay expenses for adult daycare, care coordination, and other services. This is especially important when you're single, because you may not have anyone to take care of you, and you'll have to pay for whatever care you need from your own money. It may also relieve the burden from children or other family members who might be expected to provide your care. Consult your divorce team about including the premiums for long-term care insurance in your expenses, as a part of your divorce settlement. Your CDFA™ or insurance advisor can help you research the costs, features and benefits of a policy to protect your long-term interests.

CHAPTER 11

DEBT

What you will learn in this chapter:

What is debt, marital and separate;
Types of debt;
How to divide debt;
What to do with credit card accounts;
How to protect your credit rating and your credit in your divorce.

You know, dividing our assets wasn't that much of a problem. We didn't really have that much. But we argued about money all the time. I spent too much, he spent too much, and now we have credit card bills, two mortgages, and other loans to pay back. How do we get past this?

When people think about divorce settlements, they mostly think about dividing assets- the house, cars, furniture, etc. But divorce is also about dividing debt. Money problems are often a major contributing factor to your decision to divorce in the first place. Dividing up the debt is the final step.

Most couples are very good at racking up debts of all kinds: mortgages, home equity loans, credit cards, car loans. Back in Chapter 2, we discussed reviewing your credit report. Part of the reason for this is to identify all the outstanding debt.

Another reason is to find out your credit score. Going forward, your credit score will be very important. It will help to determine if you can get a mortgage in your own name, a new credit card, make other major purchases- and if you and your spouse can each refinance the existing debt. This will help you to make decisions about keeping or selling your house and other property. Obligations you were able to maintain in your marriage may not be manageable on your own. Considering the amount of debt most couples hold, there is a lot to consider about the division of your debts that will impact your future and that of your family.

Like separate property, all debts incurred before marriage, such as personal or student loans or credit card debt you have not yet paid off, are separate debt and are yours alone.

1. **Marital Debt, if Acquired or Paid for During the Marriage, is:**

- The mortgage balance on your home and any other properties you own, and any home equity loan or line of credit balances.
- Any debts/loans you owe to banks, savings and loan associations, or any other lending institutions.
- Car loans, home improvement loans, any money you borrowed during the marriage and have not paid back in full.
- Your student loans, if not premarital. Be aware that states treat this debt differently, depending upon the specific situation. Check with your divorce team.

- Parent loans, for a child's college education.
- Loans payable to relatives or friends.
- Debt consolidation loans.
- Credit card balances: in your name, in your spouse's name, in joint name.
- Loans you have signed for or guaranteed if you own a business.
- Loans against 401(k) plans.
- Unpaid bills (department stores, doctors, dentists, etc.)

If you can, slow down on spending now and work toward clearing debts, especially if you can accomplish this with joint funds. The less you owe when you start the process, the less there is to divide in your negotiations. Consider selling some things you don't need, either to satisfy a loan attached to them, or to raise some funds to pay off other debt. If you are in financial trouble, check with a Certified Divorce Financial Analyst™, or visit an accredited credit counseling agency for assistance in figuring out your options.

If you can pay off the debt prior to your divorce, you can make a clean break, and not worry about carrying marital **debts with** your ex, post-divorce. Then you can focus on rebuilding your finances, instead of juggling payments on old debts.

Face It

Meredith took a deep breath. She had been avoiding coming to terms with their finances for most of her 15-year marriage to Derek. She simply couldn't continue to ignore the facts any longer. He had been responsible for paying the bills, but she would soon need to take that on, now that they were getting separated. She made a list of all the credit cards, and pulled up each statement online.

Then she pulled out the bank statements, and checked the balance on the lines of credit.

Thank heavens they had finally paid off the home equity loan for the new roof just last year. That left the car loans, and finally, the mortgage. She listed each item, the account number, the balance, the interest rate, and the monthly payment. You know, it wasn't as bad as she had imagined. Divided between the two of them, this was manageable.

2. Valuation Date

Many of the values we are discussing are not static. Interest accrues on debt; payments need to be made; new purchases occur. As of what date do you establish the balances that will be divided? You face the same issues as in the valuation of your assets, in Chapter 4. States have different dates that are used as the 'marker' for the debt balances.

Here are some of the choices:

- Date of Separation (a): The date one spouse physically leaves the marital residence.

- Date of Separation (b): The date one spouse informed the other of the intent to file for divorce, even if they continue living under the same roof.
- Date of Commencement: The date divorce papers are officially filed in a court of law.
- Date of a completed settlement agreement.
- Date of Trial or Distribution
- Date of Divorce

We strongly recommend that you consult with your divorce team to find the specifics for you, based on where you live, where you file, and your particular circumstances. Geography matters!

Once you are separated, debts that are run up on credit cards or loans are generally the sole responsibility of the spouse who made those purchases, unless the funds are used to pay for family needs. Keeping good records is very important here, as it is in the divorce process as a whole.

3. Types of Debt

Secured Debt:
The money owed is secured by the value of the property involved, called collateral. This includes auto loans (secured by the car), mortgages and home equity loans (secured by the house/real estate), and pledged investment accounts (secured by the investments). If you fail to pay the loan, called being 'in default', the lender can repossess or seize the property and sell it to pay off what you owe.

When calculating secured debt, the loan amount is usually offset by the value of the asset attached. For example, when taking a car worth $25,000, you also take the car loan of $17,000, making the net addition to your column $8,000. You get the car, and also the responsibility for making the remaining car payments.

If you and/or your spouse own a business, or are a key employee, you need to be aware of any personal guarantees which may be in place. Business lenders will often require personal guarantees of the owners. With a personal guarantee, the business owners (or whoever else guaranteed the loan) sign an agreement saying they are *personally* responsible for repayment. This means that a lender can pursue them if the business doesn't repay the loan. Depending on the loan agreement, they might have given the lender- often a bank- permission to take personal assets, such as your home, other property, bank or investment accounts, to pay the business loan. Even if you have not personally signed any guarantees, if your spouse has done so, jointly owned property can be at risk.

Be certain to investigate this issue thoroughly if you think it may apply to you or your spouse.

Unsecured Debt:
Unsecured debt is not collateralized. There is no property to seize if you default. This category includes credit cards, personal loans, loans from friends or family, lines of credit, etc.

Unsecured debt can be divided so each spouse receives an equitable or fair share, as you negotiate. Generally, joint debts are divided based upon who is best able to make repayment. A debt in only one name often remains the responsibility of the signer alone, depending on the use of the borrowed money. Distinctions have been made for loans taken out to purchase items for joint use, like buying a refrigerator vs purchasing a new set of top-line golf clubs. Many couples are able to negotiate this and decide for themselves who will be responsible for which debt, often with the help of a Certified Divorce Financial Analyst™, a Mediator, or their attorneys.

You are in the best position to know what will work for you in the future, and make your own decisions. If you are unable to reach agreement about dividing debts, and you live in an equitable property state, a judge will make that determination. The decision is based on a long list of factors, keeping in mind your ability to pay down the debt.

In community property states (Arizona, California, Idaho, Louisiana, Nevada, New Mexico, Texas, Washington and Wisconsin), both spouses are responsible, even for debt incurred by one partner. Alaska is an "opt-in" community property state, where spouses may agree to be jointly responsible for all debts. Puerto Rico is also a community property jurisdiction.

Credit Problems

Sheila and Dick are dividing up their assets and their loans. Sheila wants to keep the new Prius they just bought last year. It's titled in both their names and so is the car loan. Sheila was awarded the car, and the car loan responsibility with it, in their divorce settlement agreement. The judge signed off on it, with no problem.

Sheila has good intentions, but after the divorce, she just can't keep up with the loan payments. The bank collection staff calls her, and when they get nowhere, they start to call Dick. After all, he signed the loan agreement, as well. They don't know that Sheila and Dick are divorced, and quite frankly, they don't care. The late and missed car payments will damage Sheila's credit, and Dick's, too.

Dividing debts can be more complex than it may seem, as there is a third party to the transaction. You and your spouse may divide your assets as you see fit. When you divide debts, however, you are also involving the company that issued the loan, be it a bank, automotive company, or credit card company. However the two of you, and perhaps the court, choose to divide the responsibility for the debt, the creditor may follow another path if payments are not made as agreed. After all, with a joint loan/credit card, an agreement was made and signed off by both of you; the status of your marriage is not an issue for the lender. So how secure will you feel that your ex will actually pay a debt he agreed to take on?

You can agree to keep a credit card that's in joint names, and be responsible for paying off the balance. If you do not make the payments, the credit card company will come after you- and then your spouse. If you agree that your spouse will keep the house, with the mortgage and the title in joint names, you may be confident that your ex will make the payments. After all, the house is collateral for the mortgage, and he'll want to protect its equity. However, if the debt remains in both your names, it's also on your credit report, and will inflate your debt level. This could prevent you from getting a new mortgage to purchase your own home. Slow payments by your ex may have a negative impact on your credit, too. Creditors don't know, and don't care what your divorce settlement says. They just want to get paid. If your spouse doesn't pay, they will come after you.

Credit Trap

Cynthia thought her divorce from Richard wasn't too bad. They managed to take care of everything in about a year. She'd made a good transition, and was excited to buy her first new car. She was shocked when the loan was declined! She had paid her bills faithfully on time, and kept to her post-divorce budget.

When she got her credit report, she realized that the problem was Richard. He was always focused on 'Me' not 'We'! Never responsible about money (a major reason for their divorce), he had bought, well, <u>everything</u> on a credit card in her name, as an authorized user. She had forgotten to cancel it. He ran the account up to the limit and then didn't pay. The statements went to his address. She didn't even know about it.

4. So What Are Your Options?

To help protect yourself, full financial disclosure is crucial during settlement negotiations, regardless of the process you choose: Mediation, Collaborative or litigation. Make a detailed list of all account numbers, amounts owed, and who you feel is responsible for each of the debts. Ordering a copy of your credit report can help you get started. (See Chapter 2 for more information about credit reports and financial disclosures). You'll also want to obtain a copy of your spouse's credit report, to verify what debts are outstanding. Do a 'wallet search'- go through your wallet (or the bottom of your lingerie drawer) and make a list of all credit cards. Then check that list against what shows in your credit report. Be aware that it's not unusual for there to be a surprise or two here. Include this full inventory of debts with your financial affidavit. Having all accounts and balances on the record establishes a baseline of the amount of marital debt.

In Chapter 2, we suggested that you have a credit card in your name alone. If you don't have one yet, and you can, establish a new credit card account now before the divorce is final. It may be easier to qualify for a credit card based on joint income still in place, than on just your own.

After you have reviewed your credit report and that of your spouse (if you can do this together, it's much easier), cancel all unused joint credit cards, and make sure the credit card company notes that this was done at your request. Federal law does not allow a creditor to close a joint account due to a change in marital status- but you, as the borrower, can request that they do so. If you have authorized your spouse to use your credit card, revoke that authorization in writing, and ask the credit card company to issue you a new card, with a different account number.

If you can agree, and you have sufficient cash to pay the bills and sufficient credit available, contact all credit card companies, banks or other creditors to request that your joint accounts be closed or frozen, preventing any future charges. State clearly that you will not be responsible for any future charges, and follow up with a letter that puts these instructions in writing. Consult your attorney for the most effective wording. Of course, keep a copy of the letter as well as detailed notes of your phone conversations. Be sure to request that the lender report to the credit bureaus that the accounts were closed at your request.

A creditor does not have to change joint accounts to individual ones; it can require you to reapply for credit and, based on your new application, approve or deny it. That is why we suggest that you apply for credit in your own name while you are still married. Don't close your existing accounts until you have a new one in hand, just in case of emergency.

If there are balances outstanding and you have sufficient credit available, transfer the balances to your individual accounts. If the money owed is more than you feel you can handle, or if you have been left without sufficient funds to make normal purchases, simply note the balances as of the date you decide on, and make sure your divorce team is aware of this situation.

If the amount of debt is overwhelming and you can't find a way out, even with the help of credit counseling, you may need to consider filing bankruptcy. If this is the case and you are still married, both of you should file at the same time, to avoid having either one of you burdened with joint debt. Review the situation with your attorney and divorce team, and consult a bankruptcy attorney for specialized advice.

It's important that any property that still has a loan attached in joint names is either sold, paid off or refinanced into the name of whoever plans to keep it. Do not allow your name to be removed from the title before it is removed from the loan agreement- be it a mortgage, home equity line of credit, car loan, etc. You don't want to be responsible for the payments on the loan for a car you don't own anymore.

It is likely to take some time for everything to be negotiated and resolved, so first make sure timely payments are being made on all accounts, mortgages, and taxes. Don't ruin your credit, run afoul of the IRS, or put property in jeopardy during a long drawn-out negotiation.

Insist on language in your settlement agreement that states what property is to be refinanced, and the time period to complete it, along with what consequences will follow if it's not done. For example, if she remains in the family home, and is supposed to refinance it into her name alone within a year of the divorce, and she doesn't/can't do so, the home will be put on the market and sold and the proceeds divided. You can also have some of the property that will go to your ex placed in escrow until all debts are paid.

An indemnity clause in the agreement will allow you to take your ex back to court to recover any funds you may have had to pay, if he defaults on a loan and the creditor takes action against you. You can petition the court to enforce your divorce agreement. Your ex then has to appear in court to explain why the order is not being followed; he may be punished with fines or even jail time. Unfortunately, this process takes time and money.

Please note: If child support and/or alimony are needed as income to qualify for a new loan, especially with a mortgage, the lender may require that the payments be documented for a minimum of three to six months before they can be counted, and proof that they will continue for three years or more. So refinancing may not be possible for six months or more. This can be noted in the agreement.

Consult with your divorce team, CDFA™ and your attorney about these strategies, to ensure that all your debt issues are addressed.

5. **Be aware that a final decree of divorce outlines the ongoing responsibilities of your ex-spouse and yourself.**

It is not a guarantee that those guidelines will be followed. You should continue to closely monitor any joint accounts which remain open, such as credit cards, bank loans, and home equity lines of credit, during and even after your divorce. You may consider signing up with a credit monitoring service, especially if you are concerned that your soon-to-be ex-spouse might borrow money in your name. These services will notify you anytime there is a change to your credit report.

You need to remain vigilant, and check that what was promised, is actually delivered. This may be an ongoing process- but it is the best way to protect yourself and your family.

After the divorce comes the process of rebuilding. Empower yourself financially in this new chapter of your life by working with your divorce financial analyst (CDFA™) to create a budget that will allow you to establish your new lifestyle, pay your bills, maintain your credit, and enjoy your life.

For more information about Credit Reports and Credit Scores, go to: https://www.adriennegrace.com/bonuspages/.

CHAPTER 12

IS YOUR SPOUSE HIDING ASSETS?

What you will learn in this chapter:

**Multiple ways that spouses try to hide assets;
What to look for; how to find them.**

We've gone through all the financial paperwork, but it just doesn't look right to me. I know we spend more than he's declaring. Hmm. Things started to change last December, when he took a lot of cash on that 'business trip' to Barbados. They just redecorated the corporate offices. Business can't have dropped off as much as he says. And he just gave a lot of money to his mother, saying it was a loan. She doesn't need a loan! How do I get through to the truth?

When the focus changes from We to Me, behavior often takes a different turn. Goals shift from considering the benefit of the family to "How can I keep more for me, and 'give' my spouse less?"

When the National Endowment for Financial Education (NEFE), commissioned an online poll in 2015, they found that 42% of people who combined finances with their significant other have been deceptive with their spouse or partner about money. Disturbingly, this is significantly higher than the 33% who confessed to this just two years earlier in a similar poll.

39% percent say they hid a purchase, bank account, statement or cash from their partner or spouse. 6% say they lied about finances, debt, or money earned.

100% say it affected their relationship, often leading to arguments, separation and even divorce. (1)

If this is your issue, you are certainly not alone!

It is always highly recommended for you both to be open and honest with your financial disclosures. Not only is it a legal requirement, but it also makes for a much less expensive and contentious divorce, and it speeds the process along. Additionally, if a spouse *is* caught not fully disclosing assets, they will likely receive a far less than equal portion of the total marital assets, and may face penalties, perjury or other charges in criminal court.

But people will try. There are as many ways to try to hide assets, as there are creative, self-protective people. Like the song, there must be 50 ways… Here are my Top 50, listed below, generally categorized. As it's such rich territory, there is a separate section for closely-held businesses and the opportunities they offer to hide money and assets.

Again, he/she are used interchangeably.

Behavior:

1. He has become secretive about money.

2. He closely questions your spending, but will not answer questions about his own.
3. Your spouse cuts the family budget without good explanation, but does not change his spending.
4. Formerly free with cash, your spouse now pleads poverty.
5. ATM withdrawals from your joint checking account have risen in frequency and amount.
6. There are ATM withdrawal slips from an unfamiliar bank account.
7. Joint credit card accounts are cancelled without reason, notice or explanation.
8. Bank statements, credit card and investment account statements no longer come to the house, but are redirected to his office, or a post office box.
9. Your online password for the joint checking account, credit card accounts, and investment accounts no longer works.
10. Investment account balances drop without explanation.
11. A new sub-account in your spouse's name alone shows up on your investment statement and your broker will not give you details about it.
12. If you are still getting bank account statements, there's a new account number that doesn't look familiar.
13. When bank statements arrive, she whisks them away before you get to open them and review the contents.
14. A credit card statement arrives from a new company.
15. The amount of your spouse's salary drops unexpectedly.
16. Funds automatically transferred from your spouse's paycheck to your joint savings accounts drop or stop.
17. You spouse hides paystubs, or won't let you see them.

18. Instead of paying credit card bills as customary (paying the minimum due or paying the full amount as it posts to the account), your spouse overpays the credit card company, resulting in a credit balance.
19. Your spouse refuses to file income tax returns.
20. Your spouse files your joint return at the very last minute and demands that you sign the return, but will not discuss its contents, or let you or your advisors see it in advance.
21. Your spouse changes tax preparers frequently, or uses unlicensed or questionable tax preparers.
22. You think that he is cheating on your tax return.
23. Joint tax refunds, which were previously paid out, now are applied to next year's tax payments or redirected to his individual bank account.
24. Large, unexplained cash withdrawals show up on the bank statement.
25. Your spouse has not previously carried large amounts of cash, but begins to do so.
26. Spouse begins to pay cash for personal expenses that previously were paid on credit cards or by check from your joint account.
27. Spouse pays for large purchases in cash, like TV's and other large items.
28. Credit card charges show up for items you have not received: flowers, jewelry, restaurant meals, hotel rooms, entertainment, travel.
29. Spouse gives family members cash to hold, then receives 'gifts' back in return.
30. Spouse has a rapid, unexplained increase or decrease in cash or bank account balances.

31. Spouse's cellphone bill usage and charges increase dramatically; a new cellphone appears.
32. Spouse dramatically increases contributions to her 401(k) plan- or stops contributing altogether.
33. Spouse transfers a large sum of money into a custodial account for your children, or to a Trust.
34. Spouse 'lends' money to friends or family members without any documentation.
35. Spouse purchases collectibles (stamps, art, coins, guns, sports memorabilia), expensive hobby equipment for his exclusive use.
36. Spouse suddenly increases personal spending: new clothes, new hairstyle.
37. Spouse takes new interest in health and fitness, paying for fitness club membership and personal training fees.
38. You find new keys on the keyring: possibly for a safe deposit box, storage unit, residence or other unknown use.
39. Expense reimbursement checks for business travel, etc. are no longer directly deposited to your account.

In Divorce Proceedings:

40. Spouse delays providing financial information.
41. Spouse provides incomplete responses to discovery requests.
42. Spouse will not allow you, your attorney, or your divorce team access to his accountant or financial advisors.
43. Spouse threatens you with total loss of support if you request financial data.

44. Spouse threatens you with loss of custody if you request financial data.
45. Spouse stops paying normal and customary expenses.
46. Spouse makes false allegations against you.
47. Spouse ignores, or resists complying with Court Orders.
48. Spouse deliberately drives up your legal bills by stonewalling requests for financial information, forcing your attorney to make repeated requests and demands for documentation you are legally entitled to.
49. Spouse tells your children you are spending too much.
50. Spouse shows off expensive trips, new cars, or a new love interest on Facebook while pleading limited income.

Electronic Discovery

Our worlds have changed dramatically to an increasingly electronic culture. Everyone relies on their computers, tablets, notebooks, and cellphones to conduct business, including financial transactions. Deposits, purchases, statements, payments can all be done electronically. A spouse may put money in someone else's name, but may still get emails about transactions. Funds can be transferred via PayPal. New alternatives like Bitcoins, perhaps the first cryptocurrency, have no bank link, central repository or single administrator. Nobody owns or controls Bitcoin and everyone can take part.

The wording of what must be included in a financial affidavit varies by state, but it typically includes *full disclosure of stocks, bonds, retirement accounts, bank accounts and "other assets"* - and that could include Bitcoins and whatever else may arise in the future. The long delay that laws and regulations have in catching up with modern technology leaves lots of room for loopholes. Knowing that there may be a possibility for money to be hidden in new ways, in addition to offshore accounts and other known hiding places, may help you keep a sharper eye out for clues that can lead to discovery of these, and perhaps other funds as well. All transactions start with cash.

If you think your spouse is technologically adept enough to transfer money, or use Bitcoins, or hide other information on your computer, consider enlisting a digital forensic examiner, who can extract data from all kinds of electronic devices.

Computer help

When Thomas left Charlotte, he didn't take the family computer, but he deleted pretty much all the data that was in there. She had been feeling a little uneasy about things for a few months, but couldn't quite put her finger on what was wrong. When she looked around for their financial records, not only couldn't she find the files, she couldn't find the file cabinet! She knew that Thomas kept all his personal and business information on the computer, and called a forensic computer expert. He was able to retrieve the data Charlotte needed, including some accounts that Thomas 'forgot' to disclose on his financial affidavit. They were able to reach a fair settlement that met the needs of everyone in the family, and which included all their assets.

Closely-Held Businesses

If your spouse owns or is a key employee of a closely-held business, pay particular attention. The anticipation of a divorce can trigger self-protective behaviors, often well in advance of separation. These are so commonly known in divorce practice that they have tongue-in-cheek pet names: **SIDS** *(Sudden Income Deficiency Syndrome)*, **RAIDS** *(Recently-Acquired Income Deficiency Syndrome)*, **SADS** *(Sudden Asset Deficiency Syndrome)* and **MAIDS** *(Marital Acquired Income Deficiency Syndrome)*. They are all techniques to try to hide income and assets.

Although most people will honestly participate in the disclosure process, businesses provide rich opportunities to hide assets and compensation.

- Spouse's income drops just when marital difficulties become apparent. When they know divorce is on the horizon, business owners can take less income/draw because they can control their own compensation.
- When spouse prepares financial forms, income drops, but living expenses remain the same.
- The business is supposedly in trouble, but spouse's lifestyle doesn't change.
- The business pays your spouse's personal expenses and may include many current household expenses, as well.

If your spouse's business pays his personal expenses, then he doesn't need to take much of a paycheck – and can claim he has little or no income. In absorbing his expenses, the business also appears to take a hit, both in its net income and in its valuation. This can be a disadvantage unless you can carefully document what expenses the business has been paying for your household. A Lifestyle Analysis (see Chapter 4) can be of great help in this situation.

Documents retrieved

Linda, facing a divorce, knew that her husband, Zander, kept his business records at home. While he was away, she rented a business-sized copier for a day. It was a long, tedious and expensive day, but the information gathered enabled her to get an accurate valuation of his business interests, which proved to be worth a large amount of money.

More clues to hidden assets:

1. Your spouse has redecorated her office. Look for potentially expensive furnishings- rugs, artwork, antiques, that eat up business income and can easily be turned back into cash later.
2. The business has lost value since your marital problems have surfaced. It could be that your spouse has been planning your divorce for longer than you know. We often hear, *Wives plan the wedding, but husbands plan the divorce.*
3. Additional employees, perhaps friends, or a paramour, or phantoms, are added to the payroll without additional revenue being generated.
4. Your spouse is reluctant to produce bank and credit card statements, and cancelled checks for the business.

5. She stalls or stonewalls when asked to turn over financial documents, like Balance Sheets or Cash Flow Statements.
6. Vendor accounts are pre-paid, creating credit balances and diminishing cash flow.
7. He won't produce the tax returns.
8. Your spouse won't allow a business valuation by a professional. (This is likely to be ordered by the court, if necessary)
9. Bonuses, formerly paid on a schedule, are suddenly delayed. This can be arranged with a willing employer, as well as with a closely-held business.
10. Expected promotions are delayed.
11. Stock options, formerly issued at specific times, are delayed or not granted.
12. Business assets are sold/transferred to related entities.
13. The signing of lucrative, long-term contracts is delayed until after the divorce.
14. Tax Credits and Carryovers: previous year losses to be used as credits against future income, up to $3,000 per year.
15. Tax refunds are to be credited to future taxes due.

Sharing the value

Leonardo works hard in the family business. As his parents are stepping back, he and his two brothers are purchasing more of their shares, and growing both their stakes and the business itself. Last year was a banner year for the family pizza chain, with the highest sales and profits ever.

Nicole was stunned when Leonardo came home one day and asked for a divorce. Since then, he has been complaining about things slowing down, and business being bad. Leo's brother got divorced two years ago, and Nicole remembers the games they played with his income at that time. She vowed- not me! So Nicole hired the top forensic accountant in town to work on her team, to determine a real value for the business. Leo's team hired the other top accountant, and the two CPA's met to hash out the results. They were able to come up with a value that everyone could agree with. The net result: a supplemental maintenance payment to Nicole for an additional 10 years, representing her share of the value of the family business.

Specialized Help is Available

Thankfully, there is help for these situations. In addition to the work a CDFA™ and attorney do, a forensic accountant and a business valuation specialist can be of great assistance with these issues.

Why do we need to know this? A closely-held business is often the largest asset in a divorce, so an accurate business valuation is essential. If the business was started during your marriage, or its value has increased, it's usually considered a marital asset, subject to division. We can often choose between dividing the value, or viewing the business as a continuing source of income for calculating either property division, or alimony.

The only way to really unravel this web is to analyze all the financial documents with great attention to detail.

Tax returns, and other financial documents, both business and personal, must be analyzed over time, usually three to five years. A forensic accountant uses accounting skills to investigate fraud or embezzlement, and to analyze financial information for use in legal proceedings. He will try to determine if hidden income or assets exist, if business funds have been used to purchase personal assets and pay personal expenses, if the owner-spouse may have been intentionally reducing the profitability of the business and whether there have been inappropriate transactions. A thorough examination includes a detailed review of business records and practices, and internal controls, as well as issues unique to that industry. The process may produce a financial roadmap to the hidden value of the business.

Loan applications can provide good information and lead to a more accurate financial picture. It's a federal crime to knowingly provide false information to a federally insured bank, so when a business applies for a loan, there's a stronger commitment to telling the truth and looking financially strong.

If you choose to hire a forensic accountant or an investigator, let them know how much you already know. Be realistic about what you need to find out, how much money could be involved, and what it might cost to get there. Hiding money, stashing cash, concealing assets or just plain lying, can demand exhaustive measures to uncover. It can be challenging to unearth unreported income and hidden assets, but clues may be found by a trained professional. Some things may never come to light. You need to decide how far to go to look for assets you may think are there.

Don't make the assumption that your attorney will automatically look for hidden assets. You have to take a proactive role and insist there be an asset search, if you firmly believe that assets have been hidden.

Don't make the mistake of taking your spouse's word when it comes to assets. Guilt and pain can create self-defensive behavior. When it comes to getting a fair settlement, don't let emotional distress get in the way.

Anyone who lies under oath can be charged with perjury. If you find hidden assets, he can be charged. Lying during divorce proceedings is illegal. He could lose the hidden asset as a penalty for illegally concealing it from you.

A landmark in this issue is the Michigan Court decision in Sands v Sands (192 Mich. App. 698, 482 N.W.2d 203 (1992), aff'd 448 Mich. 30, 497 N.W.2d 493(1993). The defendant, Mr. Sands, hid assets during the primary trial period of his divorce. Assets were found after the trial, and the court reconsidered the property division at a new partial trial. The Michigan appellate court awarded Mrs. Sands ALL the discovered assets. It also ordered Mr. Sands to pay 70% of his wife's attorney fees, to compensate for the additional expense to uncover the hidden assets. When the appellate court affirmed the trial court's decision, it added:

'The case before us is a prime example of the burden one spouse's reprehensible behavior can impose upon not only the wronged spouse but also the court system. Under the circumstances revealed by the extensive record presented to us, we find it an abuse of discretion for the trial court not to have taken some sort of punitive action in light of Mr. Sands' persistent attempts to conceal assets...[t]hus, we find it inappropriate for the court to award Mr. Sands any share of assets that he attempted to conceal. Once a spouse intentionally has misled the court or the opposing spouse regarding the existence of an asset, that spouse should be stopped from receiving any part of that property...Accordingly, we remand...We direct the court to award full ownership of these particular assets or their equivalent value to Mrs. Sands before making an equal split of the remaining assets. This course of action should have the salutary effect not only of adjusting the equities in this case but also of serving as a warning to all divorcing parties.' xxxii.

What to Do About It

Who is the best informant, spy, source of information on your spouse's behavior? Odds are it's you! After years of marriage, you know how he thinks, who he trusts, where he might hide things and how he might do it. Think about it. Do a little creative snooping. Listen. Be aware. You may find there are clues that you have not been paying attention to. Yes, you are often the last to know. But when you stop and think about it clearly, you may be able to recall a pattern of changed behavior that can be very helpful in tracking hidden assets. Often, you can tell that a change has taken place in attitude, behavior- you *know* something is different. This may be your benchmark. Note the date (don't worry about being specific- 'around Christmas of last year' may be sufficient). Consider changes in activity, behavior, etc. from then on.   Specific questions may reveal the possibility of hidden assets, evident through lifestyle analysis, involving credit card statements, bank records, etc. Does he travel? If so, where? In what brand of hotels does she usually stay, and has that changed? Does he get an automatic transfer of funds or an allowance? Does she deposit a paycheck into a separate account?

You already know a lot of this information which can be helpful in finding what you need. Take some time and think about it carefully. Bring your notes to your team, and help them help you.

(1) http://www.nefe.org/pressroom/news/americans-confess-to-financialinfidelity.aspx.
National Endowment for Financial Education, 2/11/2016, Paul Golden

CHAPTER 13

BUILDING A DIVORCE TEAM

What you will learn in this chapter:

Who can be on your divorce team to help you handle every aspect of your journey;
Questions to ask, how to interview each specialist.

There is too much to handle!!! Michelle was at her wit's end, and panic was just a thought away. Who can deal with all these things, especially when I don't have tons of money? There's so much to do, and I still have to deal with my kids, my job- and, oh yes- my almost-ex! Help!! Who do I call?

There is certainly a lot involved in ending your marriage. In addition to the all-important family matters, you are also ending your economic partnership. This unique combination of emotional distress, physical upheaval and business matters calls for support in areas you may never have considered before. No single profession embodies the full range of skills and knowledge needed to deal with everything. Here are some of the experts you want to have on your team to help you successfully negotiate this new situation. With proper planning and help from these professionals, you can increase your chances of arriving at a settlement that fully addresses your long-term financial needs. An Attorney can help you understand your legal rights and opportunities. A Therapist can help you understand your emotions and move on to the next phase of your life. A Certified Divorce Financial Analyst™ can help you evaluate and plan for the short and long-term financial consequences of your separation or divorce. Other professionals can be consulted, as your needs may dictate.

Now is the time to see a counselor or therapist. Your world is altering around you; relationships, home, finances- all will be changed. You need a little help to manage, and to help your children manage. Seeing a counselor for 'supportive therapy' during this time does not mean you are crazy. It means you are smart enough to ask for help when you need it.

Many family law practitioners refer to divorce as a disabling condition, because most people are really not in their 'right mind' during this time. This will pass! But while you are in this situation, be sure to treat yourself with extra care. If you can, minimize some of your outside responsibilities, eat well, get some extra sleep.

Use your divorce team wisely. Don't be afraid to admit that you don't understand what an advisor or your attorney is saying to you. Divorce is a legal matter, and most of us only go through it once. Attorneys often speak 'legalese', which is not a dialect the rest of us are familiar with. When someone asks you if you understand what they just explained- resist the temptation to just nod your head. Ask for a clarification. Better yet, if possible, bring a friend or advisor to the meeting. As a CDFA™, I have often signed a confidentiality agreement, and attended attorney-client meetings, to "translate" and explain. Remember, you don't have to face this alone!

Get your divorce team in place.

Your Lawyer

You already know you will need a lawyer to handle your divorce, whether in Mediation (to review your agreement), Collaborative or litigation. Interview a few matrimonial/family law attorneys before choosing one. Look for expertise in any special aspects of your case, but also for a feeling of comfort and confidence in that relationship. You will be sharing intimate details about your marriage, sharing your past and crafting your future. A lawyer you feel comfortable with can make your journey easier.

When you hire a litigating attorney for your divorce, most communication with your spouse will stop, and the attorneys will take over. Your attorney now becomes your negotiator. Attorney personality varies- from the most reasonable to the ones known as 'pit bulls'. If it's not necessary to escalate the level of conflict, don't. The vast majority of divorce cases settle out of court anyway; few divorces actually proceed to trial.

If you are not sure how to find a lawyer, these resources can help you:

American Academy of Matrimonial Lawyers (AAML)
Email: office@AAML.org

To become a Fellow of the AAML, an attorney has to demonstrate an active interest and competency in matrimonial law, with a minimum of 10 years' experience; demonstrate that she can handle complex matters relating to custody and support of children, property division and spousal support, and also be recognized as a leading practitioner in the area of matrimonial law. These attorneys are the most experienced. They may also be the most expensive.

You can also check:

The Best Lawyers in America, under Family Law

Ask for referrals from friends, family, clergy, therapists, other professionals. The local Bar Association will have a list of divorce attorneys. Check out the attorney's website for information about experience and approach, and schedule a consultation to determine your comfort level with the individual himself.

Questions to ask:

1. Do you specialize in divorce? How long have you been practicing family law? How much of your practice is litigation? Collaborative? Mediation?

If you expect your divorce case to be contested or complex, courtroom experience will be important. Get the best representation you can afford. Keep in mind that most states provide for interim and final counsel fee awards to 'level the playing field' between the monied spouse and a spouse who may not have access to the funds.

2. How will we communicate about my case? Phone, email, letter, text or a combination? Are you available after hours or in an emergency? How long does it take to get an appointment to see you?

3. Will anyone else in your office be working on my case? What experience do they have? Can I meet them?

4. What is your hourly rate? What is the charge for the time I spend with other lawyers, paralegals, secretaries? How much is your retainer? What other costs do you expect will be involved (e.g. for private investigators, forensic accountants, Certified Divorce Financial Analyst™, physicians, vocational specialists), and how will I be charged for them? Do you have any estimate of the total cost of my divorce? Do you have payment plans? Will you bring motions in court to seek a counsel fee award if my spouse can afford more than I can?

Most attorneys use a retainer agreement that details answers to many of the questions above. 'Costs' include court and legal filing fees, as well as the expenses involved in processing paperwork.

Be wary of lawyers who charge flat fees. Even if you have what seems to be a very simple, uncontested matter, the flat fee may not cover the expenses of your case. Unexpected complications can come up, and the attorney may not wish to spend more time to get it done.

Most attorneys will avoid estimating the total cost of your divorce. There are simply too many variables involved, but it can be interesting to ask- and see how they answer.

Mediation and Collaborative Law are other choices. As out-of-court resolution processes, they are increasingly popular for divorcing couples who do not need an expensive, polarizing, highly stressful, long drawn-out adversarial process. Feel free to go back to Chapter 3, to review the different processes available to you.

If You Have Chosen Mediation

Mediation can be a challenging process. You need to find a Mediator who can provide a safe environment for you to express your concerns, and work out solutions.

Mediators have different styles, levels of experience, and varied backgrounds in law, mental health, finance or other professions. Many divorce Mediators are experienced Family Law attorneys who choose to help people come to agreement, rather than be adversarial. For others, the only background can be their own divorce experience and mediation training. Consider interviewing more than one Mediator, to find someone you both are comfortable with. Some questions to ask:

1. What is your training, background and experience? When, where, and with whom?

Although some states have certification or licensing, there is no national certification board for Mediators. Anyone who has completed a basic divorce mediation training (40 hours) can call herself a Mediator. Membership in local or national Mediation and Alternative Dispute Resolution (ADR) organizations can be a sign of experience and commitment. Writing, speaking or teaching on mediation can be also be a sign of professional recognition and skill. If he has a website, check it out.

2. What is your style of Mediation?

The Mediator's role is to listen, validate concerns, and facilitate you and your spouse to negotiate a reasonable, mutually acceptable agreement in a safe environment. In *Evaluative* Mediation, often with Mediators who are also experienced attorneys, the Mediator can give an opinion on what a judge might do with your situation in court, and offer concrete proposals for resolution of conflicts. Other Mediators use a *Facilitative* Mediation approach, assisting you to make your choices through questioning and discussion. The approaches are different, not better or worse. Ask the Mediators to discuss their approach, so that you can determine which may work best for you.

3. Are you comfortable working with other professionals, like my therapist and financial advisor, or for expertise in

business valuation, taxes, children's issues or other specialized areas?

4. What are your fees? Many charge hourly and require a retainer; others require payment at the end of each session. There may be a flat fee for preparation of the Memorandum of Understanding, the final document of the mediation, depending upon whether the Mediator drafts this document or has an attorney do so. Ask.

5. Is free consultation available? If it is, take it. Many Mediators may also charge a reduced fee for the initial consultation.

How to find a Mediator:

Referrals are always good. Family and relationship therapists and counselors are familiar with the benefits of mediation and can provide referrals. Divorce attorneys know that most divorce cases settle out of court, and that mediation can be very effective, but not all divorce attorneys are mediation-friendly. Ask your friends and family, and clergy as well.

On the web, www.mediate.com is a respected directory that provides information about a Mediator's practice, experience, and organizational connections. There are state and local divorce mediation associations. Ask court staff for a referral. Or check with your local community dispute resolution center (CDRC), where there may be free mediation of parenting disputes, and a referral list of divorce Mediators who are available on a fee basis.

If You Have Chosen Collaborative Law

Knowing that your attorney is committed to the Collaborative process is essential to the success of your divorce. A Collaboratively trained attorney will encourage clients to state their interests, rather than take positions. Agreeing to work Collaboratively at the beginning of the process requires that each of you respect the other's concerns, and work toward an agreement that addresses everyone's goals in an atmosphere of mutual respect.

Here are some questions to help you find the right lawyers to resolve your divorce Collaboratively.

1. Are you a member of any Collaborative practice groups? What types of training have you taken? When, where and with whom?

Most Collaborative attorneys belong to the International Academy of Collaborative Professionals (IACP). This is an international organization made up of legal, mental health and financial professionals working together to create client-centered processes for resolving conflict. IACP provides Collaborative training for prospective members, as well as continuing education. Collaborative attorneys (as well as all 'allied professionals') must maintain their appropriate license or certifications in good standing, adhere to their Ethical Standards, and complete a minimum of 12 hours of Collaborative Practice/Collaborative Law training.

Many areas have local practice groups, where Collaboratively-trained professionals share their experiences and provide continuing education, often under the auspices of the IACP.

2. How comfortable are you using other professionals as part of our divorce team?

The essence of Collaborative practice is that you can build an interdisciplinary team to meet the needs of your family, as well as both of you. Other divorce professionals may include Collaboratively trained:

Certified Divorce Financial Analyst™ (CDFA™) to help to clarify the financial concerns and structure an agreement that meets these needs.

Divorce coach/therapist/facilitator to help with communication and emotional issues, and keep the negotiation process on track.

Child Specialists who bring the voice of the child into the negotiations.

How to find a Collaborative attorney:

Check out the IACP website for Collaboratively trained professionals in your area: www.collaborativepractice.com. Your local bar association may have an Alternative Dispute Resolution (ADR) section which will list Collaboratively trained attorneys, as well.

Other Important Divorce Team Members:

An integral member of your team is a **Certified Divorce Financial Analyst™ (CDFA™)**. Personal finance is more complex than ever before, and divorce focuses attention on these complicated issues. You need information about financial planning, budgeting, taxation, investments, the financial aspects of divorce, maintenance and child support, retirement and estate planning, real estate and more. Developing comprehensive insight on the short and long-term financial effects of divorce can save you valuable time, money and distress. The earlier you consult with a CDFA™, the better. Financial divorce analysis helps to ensure a good, stable economic future and prevent long-term regret with divorce financial decisions. With a clear view of your financial future, you can work toward fair and reasonable legal settlement.

CDFA™s work with attorneys by helping their clients make financial sense of proposals. CDFA™s also give attorneys the tools they need to help prove their cases.

What questions to ask:

1. How long have you been practicing as a CDFA™? Do you have any other licenses or credentials besides the CDFA™ certification? Do you or your firm provide any other services (i.e. financial planning, investment management)?
2. Do you work with litigation, in Collaboration, and in Mediation? Can I see a sample of a settlement/financial plan you would provide to a client?

3. Can you work with my family lawyer, or refer me to a lawyer who can help me in my divorce?
4. How do you charge for your services, and how much?
5. What types of clients do you specialize in (i.e. women, high net worth clients)?

How to find a qualified divorce financial professional (CDFA™):

The CDFA™ designation is available to individuals who have a minimum of three years' experience as a financial professional, accountant, or matrimonial lawyer, and who complete four modules of coursework and maintain continuing education requirements. Look for a CDFA™ who is also active in the field, and for participation in professional organizations like the Association of Divorce Financial Professionals (ADFP), the Financial Planning Association (FPA), and the International Academy of Collaborative Professionals (IACP), among others.

Certified Divorce Financial Analysts™ are often also investment professionals. All licensed investment professionals have public records available online for you to review with the Financial Industry Regulatory Authority (FINRA), the Securities and Exchange Commission (SEC) and/or your state Securities Commission.

Referrals from other attorneys, therapists, friends, family and clergy are all important. You can find divorce financial specialists through the following websites, as well:

Institute for Divorce Financial Planning www.institutedfa.com

International Academy of Collaborative Professionals: www.collaborativepractice.com

Association of Divorce Financial Planners: www.divorceandfinance.org

Certified Financial Planners: www.cfp.org

Mental Health Professionals

A compassionate therapist will be an important member of your team as well. Divorce is an intensely emotional process. A support network can help you handle your fears and emotions, and focus on the financial and legal details you need to deal with. Often working with a counselor yourself can also help you to help your children deal with the changes and conflicts going on now.

During a consultation or a first visit, feel free to ask as many questions as possible:

1. How long have you been in practice?
2. What are your credentials? PhD, MSW, LMFT, LCSW, etc.
3. What is your specialty? Do you work in divorce? Collaborative practice?
4. Do you feel more comfortable with a male or female client?
5. How busy are you? How far in advance do I have to schedule a session?
6. How do you respond to a request for an emergency session?

7. Would you be willing to work with other family members if I wish to include them?
8. How much do you charge? Do you take insurance?
9. What are your office hours?
10. How long are your therapy sessions?

How to find a mental health professional:

As with most professionals, referrals from friends, family and colleagues, clergy and your other professionals are very helpful. Therapists report that the key variable that will predict a good outcome is the therapeutic rapport or connection between client and therapist. Interview a few prospective mental health professionals and see who you connect with. Marriage and Family specialists may be best suited to your needs at this time, but psychologists, psychiatrists, and social workers also can be helpful. A counselor who is included in your insurance plan may an attractive option, but divorce issues are not always covered.

You can also contact: American Association for Marriage and Family Therapy (www.aamft.org) and the American Psychological Association; also goodtherapy.org.

Your lawyer or Mediator will help you to determine what other professional expertise may help to move your case forward more quickly:

1. Vocational Expert:

A vocational expert can help you get a realistic idea of your own employability and earning potential in the current market, especially if you haven't been working outside the home in many years. This information may be used to inform the amount of spousal and child support payments, and help provide a path to employment or a better job in the future.

A vocational expert can also provide an objective, professional assessment of your spouse's earning potential. This is particularly helpful if your spouse is suffering from a case of SIDS: Sudden Income Deficiency Syndrome.

2. Business Valuation Specialist:

An accredited business valuation specialist can provide a professional estimate of the value of business interests owned, either partly or wholly by one or both spouses.

3. Forensic Accountant:

Forensic accountants have knowledge and experience in financial document analysis, accounting principles and auditing techniques. They can assist in uncovering hidden or transferred assets and income that can directly impact both support and equitable distribution.

You don't have to go through this alone!

CHAPTER 14

HOW MUCH WILL IT COST?

What you will learn in this chapter:

An overview of the fees charged by the members of your divorce team;
Other fees;
How to minimize your costs;
Tax deductibility of fees;
An option to pay for divorce representation.

Miranda sighed. We argued about money almost since the day we got married- who spent too much, on what, and why, and it's just gotten worse and worse. I've been up nights trying to figure out how to pay the bills since he moved out. I'm so sick of worrying about money, and now we have to figure out how to pay for the divorce. I want a good attorney and really need my counselor and a CDFA™ to be sure that I get a good deal. But it feels like the ultimate insult to spend money this way. If I'm going to be into budgeting now, how do I budget for this?

Arguments about money are one of the major predictors of divorce.

Spending money on getting divorced may seem like the ultimate waste of resources you need elsewhere. But achieving a reasonable and fair settlement will help bring a successful conclusion to this chapter of your life, and set the stage for the next one. Breaking up a marriage is also ending your economic partnership. Dividing assets and business interests, establishing co-parenting plans, support and maintenance arrangements- it's a lot to do. This takes expertise, and that can be expensive. Here's some information on how much it can cost, generally speaking, and how to manage some of those expenses.

Depending on your situation, expenses can range from reasonable to staggeringly expensive. The tongue-in-cheek answer to "How much does it cost?" is- at least as much as the wedding! Some uncooperative spouses just drag out the proceedings, driving up costs until you run out of money and patience. Unexpected information can surface, which may raise the level of conflict and lower the level of cooperation. An apparent open-and-shut case may change, as emotions run out of control. Or, a skilled team of divorce professionals may help you move forward with your proceedings faster and easier than you thought. Here are some tools to use to get an idea on how much this may all cost, how to minimize some of these expenses, and how to get them paid.

A wide variety of factors influence the potential cost of your divorce, including:

- ➤ Are you and your spouse able to reach agreements about the basics: Division of property, child custody, maintenance?

- Do you live in a high-cost-of-living area, with high legal fees?
- Do you have complex financial holdings, or closely-held business interests?
- How angry are you?

These factors will all influence the cost of your divorce. The more quickly and fairly you and your spouse are able to communicate and come to an equitable agreement, the less your divorce will cost to process.

Attorneys' Fees

Attorney fees are the first thing that most people think of when considering the costs of divorce, and they can be quite high. Family law attorneys, (as well as most Mediators, Certified Divorce Financial Analysts™, and mental health professionals) charge by the hour, and many take a retainer up front. The amount of the retainer is set by how much they estimate the divorce will cost, <u>minimally</u>. If more time is needed to complete your case, they will bill you to replenish the retainer; if all the time is not used, the balance is refunded. Attorneys bill in increments of time used, often by tenths of an hour, and attorney time is generally the most expensive in the mix. This includes time meeting with you, talking and corresponding with you and your spouse's attorney, traveling to and filing documents with the court, reviewing and analyzing your documents and information, needed research, and responding to emails and calls from you. Use attorney time wisely; the more issues you take to your lawyer, the higher your bill will be. Divorce attorneys are prohibited from working on contingency. They must be paid upfront, or as the case moves forward.

Whether you litigate or use Collaborative process, each of you will need to be represented by your own attorney. Even in Mediation, each of you should have an attorney review the final document before signing it. Determining how to pay these fees (Does each spouse pay their own? Are total fees divided between the spouses? Does the earning spouse pay all?) can be negotiated. When meeting with potential lawyers, be open and honest about your financial situation. Ask about the total estimated cost of your divorce, and what payment methods are acceptable (cash, credit card, installments, carrying your bill until settlement and then paying it in full out of the proceeds).

<u>Flat fee billing</u>: Some attorneys advertise that they will charge a low flat fee for a divorce. If your situation is simple and straightforward, you may be able to take advantage of this. If unexpected problems arise, you'll likely find yourself paying more than that initial fee.

<u>Task-based billing</u>: If you have a relatively simple divorce, it may be possible to take care of some portions of your divorce work yourself. This is not do-it-yourself (Don't!), but rather taking on some of the work yourself under the supervision of your attorney to save on fees. You may be able to prepare your own Statement of Net Worth, and do some preliminary negotiation with your spouse on the division of property. If

you have few assets, no children, and a short marriage, legal fees will likely be quite reasonable. You'll want your lawyer to review the agreement and point out any potential problems, no matter how simple it looks.

Mediators, who can be attorneys, or mental health professionals, or other people with mediation training, often charge by the hour, on retainer, as well. Some Mediators bill at a flat rate. Consider carefully before making a choice. When your future is at stake, the least expensive option may not be the best way to go.

Use your team to your best advantage. When you are feeing emotionally overwhelmed, or triggered by your spouse, call your counselor instead of your attorney. When you have a financial concern, call your CDFA™. Don't avoid calling your lawyer for important issues! But consider which member of the team can take care of your issue best, and most economically.

Other Fees

There is going to be a cost for filing the legal document that starts the divorce action, set by each state jurisdiction. There often is also a cost to have your spouse served (A process server hand delivers the notice of divorce to him/her), or to serve subpoenas (demands) to people who may be called as witnesses, or to provide additional information. You can often find these prices online. There is also a cost for the court reporter's time and a separate cost for any transcripts that are ordered, if your divorce proceeds to discovery or trial.

Other expenses might include preparation of quitclaim deeds to transfer property, and deed recording costs, as well as fees for the preparation of the documents necessary to transfer shares of stock, business interests, or for a Qualified Domestic Relations Order to divide a retirement account.

How Can You Minimize Your Costs?

There are ways to keep your divorce costs lower. Working to get you and your spouse to come to agreement as easily and quickly as possible helps- but make certain that you are not giving up too much in the interest of speed and economy. You only get one chance. Once the settlement is agreed to and signed, you don't get a do-over based on morning-after regrets. Getting your financial disclosure done with the assistance of a CDFA™ can often get it done faster, and more accurately, at less cost. Choose Mediation if you can, do your homework and keep an open mind, to come to an agreement as quickly as possible.

Divorce is a civil matter, not a criminal one. If you cannot afford a lawyer, the court will NOT appoint a free attorney for you. There are, however, some 'pro bono' and volunteer lawyer projects in many areas, which can provide some support for those in need.

If you are concerned that you don't have the money to retain a lawyer of comparable experience to your soon-to-be-ex's attorney, there is a possible solution. At the beginning of the divorce, your lawyer can petition the court to order that your counsel fees and costs be awarded and paid by the other spouse, either as an advance on your share of the assets, or just to 'level the playing field'. This can provide enough cash to get through the process.

When needed, seek out the assistance of family and friends.

An Unusual Solution

Amy was terrified at her situation. She had married well, very well indeed, to judge by the huge house and all the assets accumulated as Warren's career had skyrocketed. But she knew the man behind the façade, and she and their children needed to leave. However, Warren had always controlled the money. Rich as she clearly knew they were, she didn't even have a checking account in her own name. How could she hire a lawyer sophisticated enough to go up against the biggest name in town, with no money for a retainer? And Warren was furious and uncooperative. Her CDFA™ suggested she contact a divorce funding company. They were able to lend her enough money to successfully negotiate the divorce. She maintained her lifestyle and kept things relatively normal for the children during the two-year long process. The fees were then paid out of her very substantial settlement.

Bad Faith

Sometimes one spouse can make a divorce more complicated and more expensive by engaging in bad behavior, like hiding assets or refusing to provide documents or answer discovery requests: stonewalling. She may also engage in frivolous litigation by making false allegations about you, or just delay, delay, delay. If this happens, the court will often order the obstructive spouse to pay some or all of the other's counsel fees, the costs of the unnecessary lawyer work to move the case forward.

NOTE: If you are a victim of domestic abuse, and feel you cannot pay an attorney, there is help. Take your children and go to your local women's shelter (see our introduction) and help will be provided.

Divorce Funding Solutions

For wealthy couples who may find themselves asset rich but cash poor, there is an additional resource available. If there are substantial assets in the marriage (real estate, business interests, investment accounts, large retirement plans and other valuable items), but you don't have access to cash, you may be able to get a special line of credit issued by a divorce funding company. In divorces with large and complex assets and diverse holdings, the attorney's retainer can be substantial, and it may be challenging to raise the necessary cash. Proceeds of the loan may be used to pay for legal fees, forensic specialists to locate hidden assets, to value business interests, even for living expenses while the divorce proceeds.

It can help neutralize the financial advantage of the spouse who controls the money.

This is not an answer for everyone. Divorce funding companies often require combined marital assets of $2 million and up, and may have a minimum advance of $50,000-$100,000. Funding can be structured in several ways: as a loan to be paid back (with interest) upon settlement, or as an 'investment' in the divorce action, which entitles the company to recoup a percentage of the entire settlement. In the event settlement terms involve selling assets, at least one of the funding companies will work with you to facilitate the sale, and wait until it is complete before taking repayment. Divorce funding companies expect to make a profit- but they do provide a valuable service.

Of course, the settlement is reduced by the amount of funding used, but this option can enable people to achieve results that might not otherwise have been possible, and to maintain their lifestyle even through protracted proceedings.

The funding company will want to review any documents in the case: assets, business interests, prenuptial agreements, and other sensitive and private information before advancing funds. And be aware, if you reconcile with your spouse, you will likely still owe the funding company repayment of any advances.

It's not for everyone, but when this is what you need, it's great to have it available.

CLOSING THOUGHTS

"Winning" does not always mean coming in first

We're at the finish line, at last. I can't believe we have all survived this whole process, at least to here. I'm scared, and relieved, exhausted, excited, sad. I didn't get everything I wanted- but neither did my ex. I'm so happy to be here, and not at the beginning of this process any more, but I'm realizing that this is a really big, new beginning. The beginning of the next stage of my life is now here! I couldn't have done it without my team. And I'm incredibly grateful to the continuing support of my CDFA™ who will stay with me as we complete the divorce process, and begin to rebuild.

When faced with the transition of divorce, it is easy to get caught up in the quest for "winning." Winning can take many forms, from winning an argument to taking advantage of your spouse in financial negotiations. Is that really winning?

No doubt, the divorce proceedings give you ample reasons to feel mistrusting, angry, uneasy and afraid, like you are "being taken" emotionally and financially. In reality, both of you likely feel the same way. What was once a partnership is now broken. Each of you now has the burden of navigating the future on your own. Discussions move from "Where should we go on vacation next year?" to "I don't want to give up the house," to "What do I want to do next?" "We" is now "Me".

For a valuable checklist, go to: https://www.adriennegrace/bonuspages/ for the Checklist: Evaluating a Divorce Agreement.

It's time then, to redefine "winning." The truest way to win in a divorce is for both of you to leave the relationship financially stable and able to move on. When children are involved, that new definition of winning expands. It includes the assurance that their needs are met, and that the children feel they still have both loving parents. The family can be redefined rather than destroyed in the process.

If you are in the midst of a divorce, consider taking this new definition of winning to the table the next time you talk about your settlement. Being able to see both you and your spouse leave this relationship with a positive financial future truly is healthy for everyone involved.

Form your team, gather your resources, take up your courage, and move on!

Congratulations on making it through this book. You've given yourself the gift of knowledge, insight and preparation. You've put yourself in the best position to attain a fair and reasonable settlement agreement and move forward into the next phase of your life.

As you now know, it's a lot to take on! You don't have to do this alone.

My passion is helping people move through this transition successfully. As your ally and advocate, my team and I listen to your needs, help you set priorities, perform expert financial analysis, and improve your negotiation process. We empower you to reach a settlement with confidence. Whether working face-to-face in person in my office, or by Skype or Zoom or phone or via a webinar, I have the privilege of helping people answer the question, "Will I Be OK?" with: "YES!"

I have helped hundreds of people have a more secure financial life. You can have one, too.

Contact me at: https://www.adriennegrace.com

Or email me at: adrienne@adriennegrace.com for a **free consultation** to see how I can help you in your journey 'Going From We to Me".

APPENDIX 1: DOCUMENT CHECKLIST

To provide a complete and clear picture of your finances, we suggest that you gather as many of these documents as you can. Don't be intimidated by the comprehensive nature of this list. This is not the work of one day! You may not be able to locate all of these, and all may not be relevant to your situation, but having as much documentation as possible will enable your CDFA™ and your team to put together the best financial package possible for you.

Financial Data
Tax Returns – Last three years – For Client, Spouse, and Joint Personal Tax Returns
W-2s and 1099s – Last Three Years
Partnership/Corporate Tax Returns
Any Amended Tax Returns
Partnership/Corporate Financial Statements for Client and Spouse
Payroll Stubs (three most recent) for Client and Spouse
Monthly Expenses for Client and Spouse
Social Security Statements for Client and Spouse
Life Insurance Policies and Most Current Statement for Client and Spouse (Personal and through Work)
Pension Plans (Defined Benefit and Defined Contribution) for Client's Plans:
  Summary Plan Description
  Benefits Booklet

    Most Recent Statements (three years)
    Benefits Estimate:
    At Earliest Retirement Age
    At Normal Retirement Age
    At Current Age (If Eligible)
    Early Retirement Option Elections
Pension Plans (Defined Benefit & Defined Contribution) for Spouse's Plans:
    Summary Plan Description
    Benefits Booklet
    Most Recent Statements (three years)
    Benefits Estimate:
    At Earliest Retirement Age
    At Normal Retirement Age
    At Current Age (If Eligible)
    Early Retirement Option Elections
    Stock Options for Client and Spouse
    Benefits Booklets
    Most Recent Statements (three years)
IRA, Roth IRA, Keogh, SEP, 401(k), 403(b), 457 & Non-Qualified Deferred Compensation Statements for Client and Spouse
Primary Residence and Other Real Estate
    Appraisal
    Date of Purchase
    Purchase Price
    Original Mortgage Amount
    Current Mortgage Amount as of (date)
    Interest Rate/Length of Mortgage
    Monthly Payment

Second Mortgage Info

Cancelled Checks and Bank Statements for Client's and Spouse's Joint, Business, Partnership and Corporate Accounts for previous six months

Savings/Passbook Account Statements for Client's and Spouse's Joint, Business, Partnership and Corporate Accounts for previous three years

Statements regarding Securities, Money Markets, Brokerage, CDs, Commodities, Mutual Funds, Investment Accounts, Cryptocurrency, Annuities, Stocks & Bonds for Client's and Spouse's Joint, Business Partnership, and Corporate Accounts

All Employee Benefit and Executive Compensation Booklets and Statements for Client and Spouse

Wills, Trusts and Amendments or Codicils for Client, Spouse and Children

Business or Partnership Agreements for Client or Spouse

Children's Bank, Savings, Insurance and Investment Account Statements for Previous Three Years

Loan and Credit Card Statements for Client's, Spouse's, Joint, Business, Partnership, and Corporate Accounts

Listing of all individual, joint and business noninvestment assets (cars, boats, furniture, jewelry, collections, etc.)

Information on Any Cash or In-kind Transaction

Other:
_____
_____
_____
_____

_____
_____
_____
_____

Used with thanks to **Institute for Divorce Financial Analyst™**

Made in the USA
Columbia, SC
19 March 2024